PHILOSOPHY AND WORLD COMMUNITY

The series "Philosophy and World Community" appears under the auspices
of the International Federation of Philosophical Societies
and of the Conseil International de la Philosophie et des Sciences Humaines,
with the support of Unesco.

*

General Editor: RAYMOND KLIBANSKY

Copy of contemporary portrait of Spinoza

(Herzog August Bibliothek, Wolfenbüttel)

INTERNATIONAL INSTITUTE OF PHILOSOPHY

SPINOZA
ON FREEDOM OF THOUGHT

SELECTIONS FROM
TRACTATUS THEOLOGICO-POLITICUS
AND
TRACTATUS POLITICUS

edited and translated by
T. E. JESSOP

MARIO CASALINI Ltd.
MONTREAL
1962

First edition: April 1962

ALL RIGHTS RESERVED

© COPYRIGHT 1962
BY MARIO CASALINI Ltd.
MONTREAL 25, P.Q., CANADA

CONTENTS

PREFACE vii

EDITOR'S INTRODUCTION xi

THEOLOGICO-POLITICAL TREATISE 3

   PREFACE 5

   CH. III.   The Conditions of Human Security . 11

   IV.   The Distinction of Human and Divine Law 11

   V.   Civil Society and Civil Obedience . . 19

   XIII.   Scripture not Philosophical 23

   XIV.   The Nature and Content of Faith . . 25

   XV.   Faith and Reason each Autonomous . 33

   XVI.   The Natural Basis of the State. The Right to Rule and the Power to Rule 39

   XVII.   The Practical Limitations of Sovereignty 55

   XIX.   The Right of Rulers over Morality and Religion 61

   XX.   Freedom of Thought and Speech . . 69

POLITICAL TREATISE			89
CH. I.	Political Order as the Control of Human Passions		91
II.	Right and Power, Natural and Political		95
III.	The Right of the Sovereign Power over Subjects		107
IV.	In what Sense the Sovereign Power can do Wrong		115
V.	The General Characteristics of the Good State		119
APPENDIX:	FURTHER RELEVANT EXTRACTS		127
I.	From Spinoza's Letters		127
II.	From the *Ethics*		130

PREFACE

The task has been to provide a text on freedom of thought that handles the subject in a severely philosophical way. Nearly all the well-known essays either pulse with emotion or are so closely related to circumstance as to require very many antiquarian footnotes. For instance, Milton's *Areopagitica* is literature, not philosophy; Bayle, intellectual indeed, immerses himself in the detail of the contemporary controversies; and Voltaire's tracts on tolerance are generous sorties against the lack of it, not inquiries into the theory of it. J. S. Mill's *On Liberty* meets the requirement, but is easily and cheaply available, though there may be room for more translations.

Spinoza's *Theologico-Political Treatise*, austerely argued, has the special interest of setting the case for intellectual freedom in a political philosophy that emphasises the practical necessity of irresistible authority in the State, and of its correlate civic obedience. Since the informing spirit of it is as much Eastern as Western, it may be called a universal document. It is little read because its philosophical content is embedded in a mass of biblical investigations. That content can, however, be excerpted and taken independently. This is what has been done in the present volume, with the addition of cognate passages from the later *Political Treatise*, all on a scale small enough to entice students, yet omitting nothing essential.

The translation aims only at fidelity, the style of the original providing no excuse for literary pretension. The Latin text is given to make it accessible to those who have no good

library at hand, and to make the checking of the translation easy. In both treatises it is that of the first edition. The punctuation has been simplified, and the spelling adjusted to the views of present-day Latinists. For the earlier treatise I have adopted, in spite of its frequent oddity, Bruder's breaking up of the text into numbered sections, as being convenient for reference. Breaks in the numbering sufficiently indicate the omission of sections; omissions within a section are marked by three points (...). The headings of the chapters characterise the excerpts only, and are therefore my own, as also is most of the paragraphing. Having been left entirely free in the selection and translation of the passages and in the writing of the Introduction, I must ask readers to place all responsibility on me alone.

INTRODUCTION

THE MAN AND HIS CIRCUMSTANCES

Spinoza was born in 1632 in Amsterdam, of a Jewish stock that had fled from Christian persecution, first in Spain and then in Portugal [1], to the security of the Protestant Netherlands. Spanish seems to have been his mother-tongue; Hebrew was the language of his higher education, until he spontaneously moved outwards to the Latin vehicle of Western learning. A growing intellectual independence, rumours of unorthodoxy of belief, and some evident unorthodoxy of practice, led to excommunication from his synagogue and people in 1657. Soon afterwards he left Amsterdam, almost hid himself in one village and then in a second, and finally settled in The Hague (1669). Here he lived chiefly as a recluse, sometimes not moving out of his lodging for weeks on end; not, however, as a misanthrope, for when company was natural or unavoidable he behaved with the grace of a gentleman. His dominating desire was to pursue his philosophical and scientific studies, which he habitually continued well beyond midnight. To ensure freedom for them he was content to live in decent poverty, accepting no post, and providing for his few wants by grinding optical lenses, an occupation that prompted Heine's charming (though false) remark that all subsequent philosophers had seen through the glasses which Spinoza had ground. His sedentary labours and abstemious ways, supervening on a

---

[1] His name was Portuguese, Bento Despiñoza, which he later latinised into Benedictus de Spinoza. Religiously he had borne the equivalent Hebrew forename Baruch.

predisposition to consumption of the lungs, brought about his death at the early age of forty-four (1677).

Although the externals were so modest, the man himself was widely known: the testimony of his earliest biographers is to some extent confirmed by his surviving correspondence. The secretary of the recently founded Royal Society of London, Henry Oldenburg, exchanged letters with him, and conveyed his name and ideas to English scientists. Among those who called on him was Leibniz. In 1673 the Elector Palatine offered him a Chair at Heidelberg University. Within his own land he had the fame of public disfavour, through the powerful hostility of the ecclesiastical authorities. Because of this he held back his chief work[1], the gathered fruit of all his philosophical thinking, to which he gave the deeply right, though inadequately descriptive, title *Ethics*. When published after his death (by his direction), it was condemned as irreligious because it departed from all the several orthodoxies. For a full century he was known as "the atheist", and was not allowed to muddy the currents of thought either on the Continent or in Britain. Then the Germans Lessing and Herder, penetrating below the form and letter of his writings, revived and cleansed his reputation; Jacobi, Schleiermacher, Hegel and Schelling brought him back into philosophical circles, supported in England by Coleridge; and since then he has been ranked among the classic metaphysicians of the West, with a niche apart as almost unequalled in elevation of character and conduct.

What contact did so retiring a scholar have with his country's affairs? Did he write about political philosophy with only a bookish knowledge of the subject? And why did he make his political philosophy an argued plea for freedom of intellectual discussion? Something, however little, must be said about his country that is relevant to these questions.

In 1648, when Spinoza was a lad of sixteen, the seven Protestant northern provinces of the Netherlands successfully ended an eighty-years' struggle to free themselves from Spain. Each province was formally a sovereign power, with its own

---

[1] See Ep. 19, below, p. 128.

assembly; the Republic of the United Provinces operated through an assembly called the States-General, consisting of delegates of the provincial assemblies. Not surprisingly, the recurrent internal problem was how to conciliate federal and provincial interests. Those provinces that were controlled by the well-to-do burghers jealously guarded provincial autonomy. Among them was Holland, easily the most important of all the seven (it included the cities of Rotterdam, The Hague, Delft, Leyden, Haarlem and Amsterdam, this last one of the richest in the world), so that its delegates usually had the dominant voice in the States-General. Opposition to the particularist policy came from the clergy; also from the ordinary people, who were inadequately represented in the States-General, and were emotionally attached to the successive Princes of Orange, because of the military leadership these had given in the long war for liberation. These princes had no constitutional position in the Union except that of being its occasional servants. The controversy between the Unionists and the Provincialists was thus complicated with the clash between an ecclesiastical and a lay view of the use of State power, the claims of the poorer citizens against the wealthy burghers, and the question of the possible constitutional supremacy of the House of Orange.

It was in the strong province of Holland that Spinoza lived out his whole life. From 1653 the leader of its assembly, and also of the States-General, was Jan de Witt, a statesman of great ability. For almost twenty years he held the reins of government. Then, blamed for a failure in foreign policy, he fell, and met a horrible death at the hands of a mob (1673)[1]. Curiously, Spinoza was acquainted with him, received a pension from him, and (we learn from Leibniz) was overwhelmed with grief and anger at his assassination. When the acquaintance began, how close it was, and what occasioned and perpetuated it, are not known. The earliest biography of Spinoza

---

[1] In the *Tr.-Pol.*, IX, 14 *ad fin.*, Spinoza gives an impersonal explanation, in terms of a defective constitution, of this ending by the Orangists of oligarchic rule in the United Provinces.

(attributed to Lucas) says that De Witt "often did him the honour of consulting him on important matters"; and a contemporary pamphlet alleged that the *Tr. Theol.-Pol.* was written to give support to De Witt's internal policy. There being no room to examine these points and very little evidence to help, it may be safest to say, first, that his knowledge of political principles does not seem to require any external explanation; secondly, that such knowledge as he shows of the human difficulties of political administration could, in a small country, have been got by any educated citizen, without access to the confidences of a statesman; thirdly, that his occasional remarks about the superiority of a republican constitution could plausibly be taken as confirming De Witt's constant care to keep the House of Orange from rising to supremacy; and lastly, that his emphasis on a religious and intellectual freedom guaranteed by both the law and the power of the State was in harmony with De Witt's policy of refusing to use the arm of the State for the imposition of controls and penalties demanded in the name of God by preachers and ecclesiastical synods.

Formally, by the terms of the Union of Utrecht of 1579, the United Provinces stood for freedom of religious profession and worship. It was statesmen like De Witt who maintained that provision, against the Dutch Church. This, being Calvinist, had a tightly organised theology, and in Calvin's Geneva had a precedent for imposing both its doctrine and its discipline through the instruments of political authority. Spinoza makes a warning mention (below, p. 84) of such an imposition in the United Provinces. In 1610 a section of the clergy, led by Jacob Harmens ("Arminius"), having suffered some opprobrium for dissociating themselves from the doctrine of predestination, had appealed to the assembly of the province of Holland in a "Remonstrance" (hence the name Remonstrants; Arminians is a later name). The dispute passed higher to the States-General, which resolved to seek a solution by summoning a national synod of the Church, the delegates of Holland vehemently leading the dissident minority, resenting the interference of the federal assembly in the affairs of a province, and fearing the possibility of a political restriction of religious

Autograph letter from Spinoza to L. Meyer, 3 Aug. 1663
on the latter's draft of a Preface to Spinoza's
Renati des Cartes Principia Philosophiae

(Bibliothèque Victor Cousin, Sorbonne)

freedom. The synod met at Dort in 1618, in the next year condemned the Remonstrants, and deprived them of their posts. In the meantime the States-General had taken political action: some members of the dissident provincial assemblies were expelled, and Holland was handled with special severity, its leader being executed and two of its prominent men sentenced to imprisonment for life—one of them the jurist Hugo Grotius, who managed to escape to Paris and never again saw his native land [1].

This episode, and the continuing political influence of the Calvinist clergy, formed the local background of Spinoza's plea for toleration. He was aware that further afield Romanists were oppressing Protestants, and where the latter had triumphed one of its sects was oppressing the others, the issue almost everywhere being not whether brain and conscience should be free, but which Church or sect should be the spiritual ruler of the nation, since each passionately believed that it alone had the truth. More intimately, there was the memory of his own expulsion from the Jewish community (borne magnanimously), and doubtless, surviving this, a sense of solidarity with his forbears, brands plucked from the burning in Spain and Portugal.

HIS POLITICAL PHILOSOPHY

The *Tractatus Theologico-Politicus*, begun by 1665 [2], was published anonymously in 1670. It was condemned by Calvinistic synods in the same year, was prohibited by the Court of Holland in July 1674, and soon appeared on the Roman Index. The *Tractatus Politicus*, unfinished, appeared in 1677 in Spinoza's *Opera Posthuma*.

The later treatise begins with a compact exposition of his political philosophy, and then proceeds to the not obviously philosophical business of proposing model consti-

---

[1] Spinoza's library at his death included a copy of Grotius's *De imperio summarum potestatum circa sacra*.
[2] See Ep. 30, below, p. 127.

tutions for the monarchic, aristocratic and democratic types of State (only a few pages on the last, his pen being stopped by death). It does little more than mention the view of the relation of religion and philosophy, and the plea for freedom of thought and teaching, that have an emphatic place in the *Tr. Theol.-Pol.*

In the earlier and much longer treatise the strictly philosophical argumentation breaks out intermittently, most of the space being taken up with a close exegesis of the Bible, chiefly of the Old Testament, on which Spinoza wrote as a master. His main purpose was confessedly to develop a case for liberty of rational inquiry, and because the age was a religious one it was the religious leaders he had to confront. Descartes had had to do the same: he underpinned his purely scientific (and therefore secular) cosmology with an epistemology and metaphysic that justified both it and, he hoped, the theological orthodoxy watched over by the doctors of the Sorbonne. Spinoza, in a land of Calvinists, had to address more biblically minded scholars and theologians. He selected and bent his large biblical material to the conclusion that religion and philosophy are so different in aim and method that there is no reason why they should clash.

In that predominating context the questions of political philosophy seem to arise subordinately. It could be argued that Spinoza was an unorthodox thinker who simply wanted freedom for himself and all other trained thinkers; that he saw that the demand raised the issue of the extent of political authority; and that, precisely because he was a philosopher, he pushed the issue back to the examination of the very *raison d'être* of the State. I would demur only at the restrictive word "simply"; for both treatises breathe a warm, if not primary, interest in the human distress of his day. Religion and politics, both vehement, were inseparable, as much in Protestant as in Romanist countries: whichever of the two interests was touched brought the other into play. The result was either civil disorder, or civil order secured by oppression. Spinoza saw both as painful, debilitating, and debasing, and sought a theory that would indicate and ground a way of avoiding them.

The human plight and the need for a State. The starting-point and first few steps of the theory are extreme simplifications, to be modified later. Human nature, selfish enough under political controls, would be disastrously so without these. This is Spinoza's basic presupposition, seen as a special instance of a universal law which he posited in his metaphysical system, namely, that every individual thing whatever has a necessitated urge to persist in the manner of existence proper to its kind (*perseverare in esse suo*)[1]. That every man seeks his own survival and satisfaction is thus a necessity of nature, and consequently to be neither deplored nor condemned: theorists can only draw out its implications, and rulers must take it into account. The immediate implication is that men in physical proximity, if without external restraints, would inevitably be hostile to one another. In the struggle each would be his own and sole judge and guardian. There would be no bodily security, no property in the sense of entitled possession, none of the amenities that arise from co-operation, and no morality, since no one could count on the *reciprocal* recognition of duties. Everything would be in constant jeopardy, including life itself.

Selfishness, constantly frustrated, would become intolerable, and intelligence, in the service of self-interest, would seek a way out. A simple agreement to regulate rapacity and unscrupulousness in order to get the benefits of peace and security would be futile because of the absence *and impossibility* of trust. No arrangement could operate unless it were irresistibly enforced; and enforcement would be possible only if every individual surrendered to one body (an individual or a group) not only his natural freedom of action, thus giving that body the *right* to rule, but also, and at the same time, everything needful to give that body the *power* to rule; for

---

[1] An old doctrine. Cp. St. Thomas: " There is in man an innate inclination to seek his own natural good. In this respect he is like all substances, for each of these strives to preserve itself in its distinctive form. Accordingly, what preserves human life and what hinders the destruction of it are covered by Natural Law " (*Summa Theol.*, pr. sec., qu. 94, art. 2).

in the order of nature right extends only as far as power[1]. The wills of all, so far as action is concerned, have to give way to a single will, and the powers of all, mutually limiting and destructive when used by every man severally, have to be pooled and lodged firmly in the possession of that one will.

This looks like merely another statement of the old doctrine of a social contract. But it differs in an important respect. The old version assumed an original social cohesion, so that a contract was needed only to account for a *politically ordered* society. Spinoza's version (taken, with much else, from Hobbes[2]), resting on the denial of a spontaneous social unity, was that a society (in the proper sense of a fellowship) and a State could only arise simultaneously, being factually identical.

In the *Tr. Theol.-Pol.* he usually writes as though there had in fact been a wild freedom that was found to be no freedom, and in fact a compact as the sole escape from wretchedness (in the *Tr. Pol.* a compact is only mentioned in passing). It is possible that he believed the result of his imaginative stripping away of imposed restraints to have been once upon a time a reality; but in view of the abstract and deductive cast of his mind it is more likely that he was not so much guessing how States originated as inquiring what makes the State an abiding necessity, was much less concerned with any temporal beginning than with the justifying ground in human nature of the fact and requirements of political order.

Sovereignty as absolute. In the sixteenth century the notion of an ultimate political authority had acquired, through the

---

[1] Spinoza's use of "natural right" is eccentric: it stands not for an entitlement but for a brute fact, for the free course of a man's nature-determined appetites and passions, subject to no check except the similar appetites and passions of others. The Sovereign Power, as the very fount of law, has and needs no civil rights; as created by the surrender of the natural "rights" of the ruled severally, it has and needs only natural "rights", subject to no external check except such collective power as may *in fact* remain with the people. For Spinoza, then, a natural "right" is an actual power of action.

[2] From the *Elementa philosophica de cive*, 1647, a copy of which was in Spinoza's collection of books at the time of his death. Also in this were the works of Machiavelli, whom Spinoza mentions appreciatively in *Tr. Pol.*, V *ad fin.*

French jurists, the name Sovereignty. Spinoza, writing in a Latin that was mostly classical in its vocabulary, chose the expression *summa potestas*, which I have usually rendered "Supreme Power" because he presses the literal sense of both words. He makes it stand for the concrete sense of Sovereign as well as for the abstract sense of Sovereignty, and allows that the Sovereign may be, according to accident, custom or need, an individual, a relatively small group, or the whole body of the people. Where Sovereignty *ought* to reside is not Spinoza's overt concern (though he confesses a preference for democracy). What comes to the fore in his exposition, with a strong repetition like the beating of a drum, is an insistence that there must be Sovereignty somewhere. State and society are correlative ideas.

Spinoza proceeds to a logical elucidation of the notion of Sovereignty, and then to the application of it, in which it becomes evident that a pure notion and an embodied one cannot be quite the same.

Since Sovereignty as a notion means supremacy, it is absolute. Limitation has no place in it. If it were qualified in any way, it would be destroyed; if it were divided, the parts would limit one another, so that there would be supremacy nowhere; and if it were alienable, possessed under conditions that enabled it to be withdrawn, it would be subordinate, not supreme. By its very meaning it is unlimited, indivisible, inalienable. If it is to exist, it must be given absolutely and possessed absolutely. The compact logically required to ground it (and perhaps causally required to create it) must be conceived accordingly. When there is no single and unfettered source of laws, decrees and enforcement, there is no Sovereignty, no State, no society, but only chaos, rapine, violence, and brevity of life, with no chance of rising to civilised aims and achievements.

Order or security being the purpose of the creation of Sovereignty (which is thus a means, not an end in itself), it is the paramount principle of government. In other words, the utterly essential test of the methods and extent of the Sovereign's rule is their *causal effectiveness* for that end. The material in which the end is to be achieved is refractory.

As for methods, they are to be suited to beings that, besides

being egoistic, are impelled by passions. This entirely natural fact makes them incapable of living by that spark of reason with which they detected their need of a common control; that is, although the compact (explicit or implicit) rests on reason, they have not enough reason to maintain the compact voluntarily. Therefore the complete subjection to which they are committed in their own interest must be assured by methods addressed to their passions. Since these are at bottom either recoil from hurt or lust for benefits, the Sovereign will procure obedience by appealing when necessary to fear through threats of punishment, and when possible to hope through promise of reward. In both cases the subjects are given an obvious self-interest in obedience. When conditions allow of more appeal to hope than to fear, obedience will be easier. Fear alone blinds subjects to the benefits of compulsion; but most men cannot be always obedient without it.

As for range, no area of external conduct is in principle outside the sovereign jurisdiction, because any part of it may become prejudicial to the public order. In consequence, the Sovereign has to decree what is morally right and what is morally wrong in their *specific and overt* applications; and to control the institutions and external requirements of religion, again not to display authority but as a causally necessary way of restraining factious passions and of preventing the possibility of an ecclesiastical *imperium in imperio*.

Spinoza is saying that wherever Sovereignty lies it must have whatever power it needs to fulfil the difficult task, the prevention of primitive anarchy, which justifies its existence. That, and not abstract considerations, is the principle of dominion. It follows that the only wrong a Sovereign can do, *qua* Sovereign, is to command or perform anything that would weaken or break his *power* to maintain public order. When a ruler, for whatever reason, becomes powerless to rule, the people no longer have any motive for obedience: the compact having in effect lapsed, they resume their "natural" freedom, which they may either riot in, to their hurt, or surrender to another ruler of their own creation.

Spinoza's theory of the absoluteness of Sovereignty is, then, a grim one. It pins us down to the choice of either the miserable

anarchy of "natural" freedom or the total loss of freedom. The latter, he tells us, is the lesser evil. His meaning, translated into the simplest language, is that we have greater need of protection from one another than from an irresistible governing power. This, however, is only the first stage of Spinoza's exposition. He has been laying down fundamentals. As a scientist and philosopher, with a passion for logical order, he has the mental habit of first clarifying a problem by clearing away all complications. When he introduces these, the prospect changes.

The limits of Sovereignty. Although Sovereignty is unlimited in principle, it is not so in practice. A people cannot in fact be made to submit to anything and everything. Despotism, Spinoza remarks (quoting Seneca), does not last long. The laws of human nature are against it. There are some things which the Supreme Power cannot do, some which it would be sheer folly to do, and some which it would be undesirable to do.

There are natural impossibilities. Only outer acts can be controlled by commands and force; what goes on in the mind is beyond the reach of coercion. True, hopes and fears can be aroused, but what men hope for and fear cannot be wholly determined from outside, nor whom they love and whom they hate, nor what they think, and what they judge to be true, right, or expedient. The Power's power can secure only external conformity.

Another limit is set by elementary prudence. That in certain conditions obedience cannot be relied on is a law of human nature, and an obvious one. A Sovereign that presses the people to the point where they will rebel is not necessarily immoral but is certainly foolish; for the unity and stability of the State are as much his (or the ruling group's) interest as theirs, and his own selfishness as well as theirs will be unsuccessful if rule collapses. Spinoza here repeats the ancient saw that despots fear their subjects more than these fear them. The basic justification of Sovereignty is that it replaces the pains and dangers of wild freedom with the security of a regulated freedom, and if what men get is all regulation and no freedom they will break loose. It requires subjects, but not slaves. That

justification prompts Spinoza to glance approvingly, in an aside, at democracy. The State being for freedom, the best State will be one that most secures the most freedom, and will therefore be one in which the people surrender their individual liberty of action to themselves collectively, exercising the Sovereignty thus created through an assembly that is accountable to them in their collectivity; for then, while obliged to submit to the laws, they are but submitting to themselves [1], thus being truly citizens, never merely subjects, and never slaves. But Spinoza does not press this; it is a theoretical implication. He believes that the degree of freedom that can in practice be granted does not depend on the mere form of government.

The two kinds of limits can both be interpreted within the narrow framework which Spinoza, for logical simplicity, laid down at the beginning, namely, a minimal view of human nature and a consequentially minimal vindication of the need for a Sovereign Power restricted only by the natural laws of cause and effect in human nature. His aim, in accordance with his metaphysical determinism, has been to study political life with the dispassionateness of a scientist. He has tried to think in terms of the verbs "is" and "must", with "ought" allowed in its prudential, not its distinctively moral sense. There *must* be Sovereignty *if* there is to be a State; and the Sovereign Power *must* recognise certain limits *if* the State is to be maintained. These are not to be read as moral imperatives, but as statements of inviolable natural laws.

Nevertheless, in his treatment of the limits of logically and legally unlimited Sovereignty [2], Spinoza introduces what

---

[1] As Rousseau was to say nearly a century later. Marsilius of Padua had said much the same 350 years before Spinoza: "In obeying laws to which all men have agreed, all men are really governing themselves".

[2] That the Sovereign is above the law was a principle of Roman Law — *princeps legibus solutus est*. St. Thomas limits its meaning: "A ruler is said to be above the law so far as its *coercive force* is concerned; for law derives its coercive force entirely from the power of the ruler, and nobody can be coerced by himself" (*Summa Theol.*, pr. sec., qu. 96, art. 5).

seems to be downright moral judgment. The change of plane becomes obvious when he begins to insist that the members of a political society are, after all, *humans*, beings of a peculiar kind. As part of their humanity they have moral and religious convictions. These also have to be taken into account by the political theorist and by the Sovereign, and, by the former at least, not merely as facts. Spinoza is now widening his area of reference, correcting his first abstraction, by recognising that men are not merely lusting, rapacious and pugnacious animals. The importance he assigns to public peace and order seems to be as much one of moral need as of passional craving, and beneath his artificial language of " natural freedom " and of a " compact " he is suggesting that freedom is something to which humans are *entitled*, in a more than contractual sense. When he says that the " highest " principle of civil law is the welfare of the people, he does not appear to mean either the most general logically or the most effective causally, but the most authoritative morally. When writing about the utterly inevitable State he sometimes lets fall a remark about the *good* State; in the *Tr. Pol.* he investigates the *good* forms of monarchy and aristocracy; and in neither case does he reduce " good " to " stable by any means ". As we shall see shortly, he brings in charity, and does so not only as a causally inducible attitude that is useful for public harmony, but also as a virtue, not a mere fact but an excellence; and he presses his plea for liberty of intellectual inquiry as something that is involved in man's " true good ".

His final view of man and of the State shapes itself on this plane of aspiring considerations. The abstract, hypothetical wild man (a *Grenzbegriff*) gives place to something like the man we know: human nature is not incorrigibly non-social and non-moral, but its social and moral possibilities have no chance of development in circumstances of primitive struggle. Such sensibilities, useless and hurtful when nobody can be trusted to reciprocate, are able to operate and become habitual when everybody is under the equal discipline of imposed laws. The State, at first conceived as enforcing the sole conditions of survival, security, and collaboration for material satisfactions, is now conceived as providing also the conditions under which

alone morality, religion, and intellectual pursuits can unfold themselves, and at the same time ensuring that they do so without hurt to the public order, indeed to its great advantage, since humanised men have motives to lawabidingness that lessen considerably the need for the use of coercive power, a power remaining indeed with the Sovereign but capable of being, for such men, held largely in reserve. Coercive laws, so long as they are required, are educative, bridling the passions, making right action habitual, enabling some men to become aware of their capacities, and supplying the reliable framework within which these can be brought into play. Spinoza goes so far as to say that precisely because the firm rule of a Sovereign Power alone makes morality realisable, obedience to that Power is the highest moral law.

The moral nature of man adds limits to the natural and prudential restrictions on Sovereignty[1]; but Spinoza prefers to say positively that a politically ordered life adds moral possibilities to the lower necessities of human nature. Further, he places the causal responsibility for distinctively human advancement on the governing, not the governed, side of the State: if a people is bad, he says, the rulers cannot be ruling well, are not recognising that most men cannot move up the ladder towards the higher ends spontaneously, but have to be trained by suitable restraints and encouragements. In the broad metaphysical sweep of the *Ethics* the State appears as one of the conditions of man's redemption.

Freedom of religion and philosophy. Our beliefs about God, our devotional attitudes, and our conclusions about what is true and what false are untouchable so long as they remain within the privacy of our minds. So far we need no liberty; we have it by nature. When, however, we express them outwardly, in speech or action, we bring ourselves within the jurisdiction of the Sovereign Power. What freedom can the latter grant here, consistently with the public peace?

---

[1] Cp. Epictetus's imaginary conversation with a bullying magistrate (*Discourses*, III, vii. 32): "I can throw anyone I wish into prison". "As you can a stone". "And I can flog anyone I wish". "As you can an ass. This is not governing men".

The conclusion of Spinoza's lengthy examination of the Bible in the *Tr. Theol.-Pol.* is that religion consists essentially in belief in God and worship of Him in the form of loyalty to His moral requirements. The fruit and proof of it are the two virtues of justice and charity, *i.e.* respecting the rights of others and acting benevolently towards them. Behaviour as so characterised is plainly appropriate to human nature, and powerfully helpful to the maintenance of the political bond. A State without it is less unified, and therefore less truly a State, than one with it. But religion has gathered about itself historical accretions of ceremonial requirements and far-ranging doctrines, and differences of opinion about these have produced a variety of sects. All of these can be tolerated by the State if and so far as they demand and produce the essential virtues of justice and charity. But so far as the differences divide subjects (as they notoriously have done) into mutually suspicious and rival and hostile groups, the end of the State requires them to be forbidden open expression. Again if that end is to be preserved, no religious group is to be allowed to claim, or by any means acquire, the political power to impose on the citizens its peculiar doctrines, usages and discipline. The religious freedom of the individual stands internally because it cannot be touched; it stands externally in the form of justice and charity, if the State protects these.

Is there room for freedom to philosophise? That is, with open utterance in speech and print, since the inner activity is inviolable. Here Spinoza comes at last to what he calls the main purpose of the *Tr. Theol.-Pol.*, namely, to show that religion and philosophy are so distinct as to be compatible. He shaped his argument in this way because the objections to unrestricted philosophising came in his day (as often before and since) from ecclesiastics, theologians and preachers. He concludes that the objections are misconceived. Religion has its great place as belief in one God, in and through whom all things have their being, who is to be worshipped inwardly with devoutness and outwardly with the practice of justice and charity. All further views about God, man and the world are matters of intellectual inquiry, in which nothing can be imposed. As for the Jewish and Christian Scriptures, it is plain

that they are not philosophical documents: they were written in the thought-forms of the times to which they belong and, being intended for the people generally, were clothed in language that had meaning and appeal for everybody. Their constant theme is loyalty to God, not intellectual understanding of Him. The aim of religion is practical — piety and morality, to remove wickedness, not theoretical ignorance. The aim of philosophy is truth, knowledge perfectly clarified and ordered. The one calls for faith and obedience, the other for reasoning. The two are entirely distinct in goal, attitude, method and criteria. Each is autonomous in its own sphere, and therefore a usurper if it tries to dominate the other.

In the context of political philosophy the question at issue is whether the Sovereign Power, as the sole guardian of peace and welfare, can *wisely* allow the cry of heresy to be raised against philosophers, and give the support of law with its sanctions. More broadly, should there be laws against opinions and theories? The answer is to be in terms of those twin political principles, the minimal one of peace and the supervening one of larger and higher welfare. Spinoza notes that there are opinions that contravene these, and therefore have to be made punishable — *e.g.* seditious ones, which attack either Sovereignty or the Sovereign, thus striking at the very foundation of publicly ordered life; those that incite to illegal acts; and those that are directed by such passions as anger and revenge.

Such clear exceptions apart, laws against the open expression of opinions are not in the public interest. Indeed, to a certain degree they are futile, and therefore simply foolish, for nearly everybody sometimes, and some people often, cannot help blurting out their views. If the laws could be rigorously enforced, the result would be that a large part of the people would speak in one way and think in another, a duplicity and veiled disloyalty that could not be good for any State. In practice, laws against certain opinions become themselves causes of dissension. They originate not usually with the Sovereign, but with a sect or party that has persuaded or pressed the Sovereign to protect their doctrine and influence; and it is the leaders of such ambitious and intolerant groups that are the actual schismatics, for under the cover of the law they

spy out dissentients, rouse the populace against these, initiate prosecutions, and force them through. Further, laws against opinions strike hardest against men of considered convictions, men whose moral or intellectual integrity will not allow them either to be mute or to trim their speech to an imposed orthodoxy; for weak characters can conform with ease, and hotheads need no punishment for their speech because they usually run into punishable actions. When the strongest-minded men are punished merely for saying what they honestly think, a premium is placed on the weak and the hypocritical. This may, for a while, procure the appearance of peace, but it will not favour human advancement. It is not a bare possibility but a fact that forbidden opinions are held, and with honourable intentions uttered, by men of blameless life, just and benevolent and loyal in spirit as well as in behaviour. In what sort of a State can *these* be publicly disgraced as criminals, and thrust into dungeons or sent to stake or block? The function of Sovereignty is turned inside out when any subject is judged not by his deeds but by his words and views.

It is sensible, therefore, to acknowledge the individual need and the social advantage of free speech by making it, within easily definable limits, a civic right. Neither morality nor religion will suffer; nor will the peace of the State — on the contrary, the State will gain a wholeminded loyalty.

This culminating conclusion of the *Tr. Theol.-Pol.* can be read as a plea for allowing all non-seditious and non-inflammatory discussion. In the light of the contemporary situation in the United Provinces it can be read as a veiled justification of the domestic policy of Jan de Witt and his party, which was one of liberal toleration in matters of religion, and of keeping the conduct of political affairs outside the pressure of ecclesiastical interests [1]. When, however, the brief final argument is

---

[1] It is so read by C. Gebhardt (Spinoza, *Lebensbeschreibungen*, 1914, Leipzig, p. 142) and by B. Alexander (*Spinoza*, 1923, Munich, p. 67). J. Freudenthal, in his *Spinoza, Leben und Lehre* (2nd ed., ed. by C. Gebhardt, 1927, Heidelberg, p. 129) quotes from a pamphlet of 1672 that the *Tr. Theol.-Pol.* was " published with the connivance of Mr. Jan de Witt and his accomplices ".

read, as it surely must be, as the sequel to that large part of the treatise which is occupied with displaying biblical grounds for the thesis that religion and philosophy are mutually independent, Spinoza's case for freedom seems to be rather the plea that *philosophers* should be given the protection of the State against molestation by ecclesiastical tests of orthodoxy. This is borne out by the sub-title of the treatise and by Ep. 30 (below, p. 127). He has been at some pains to show that the rational study of the universe can proceed by no tests except those of reason and fact, and makes the pragmatic point that only when left so to proceed can it promote the sciences and the useful arts, rich in social benefits. He admits the implication of his own political philosophy that philosophers as citizens must submit to the laws of the State, but urges that, whether or no they inwardly approve of this or that particular law, they can obey it willingly because they understand more fully and more constantly than most men the sheer necessity of general and enforced law. He urges also that the very mentality that makes them philosophers makes them peaceable: reasoners tend to be tolerant of one another because they know that reasoning is difficult, because they expose their findings for examination by acknowledged criteria, and because their only ambition is to detect truth. They are not likely to inflame or corrupt the multitude, since they address their writings to one another, in technical form and for the most part in the Latin tongue [1]. To all which Spinoza adds the moral plea that reasoning is the highest and rarest of all virtues, the mind operating in its most peculiarly human way, without passion and with clearness and cogency. On these various grounds he makes his ultimate declaration that any State that silences the relatively few men who possess the gift and use of reason, or allows them to be the victims of heresy-hunts, is denying itself the full service of its most reliable citizens.

---

[1] Spinoza prevented the publication of a Dutch translation of the *Tr. Theol.-Pol.* See Ep. 47, below, p. 127.

INTELLECTUAL FREEDOM AS A POLITICAL PROBLEM

Since a philosophical text is to be read not to put thinking to sleep but to exercise it, some comments may be offered on Spinoza's main problem, leaving the rest unexamined. If long titles were not a nuisance, the title of the present volume should have been " Spinoza on the Rights of Government and the Rights of Intellectual Thought ", since this does justice to his directive idea that there are *two* sets of rights. In his abstract way he is trying to do justice to the concrete human situation.

What are we to mean by the rights of rulers? That certain men have an inherent title to control the lives of millions of their fellow-men? So Plato held. Some men are certainly better fitted than others for that office; but their superior fitness, regarded in abstraction from particular circumstances, appears to entitle them not to the office but to eligibility for it. If this be so, the rights of rulers, whether strictly sovereign or no, arise not from themselves but from their office or function: however they became rulers, they must have the *powers* necessary for the discharge of the office. This is a causal law, and a moral one too, since it is obviously *unfair* to expect a person (individual or corporate) to perform a duty without the requisite means. What the office is in detail, and therefore what powers it calls for, are matters for investigation, since they vary with circumstance; but the law looks very like an axiom.

The rights of subjects, on the other hand, do not arise out of an office in the sense in which ruling is an office. Those that have been publicly granted, *i.e.* civic rights, are thought of primarily not as powers but as *liberties*, protected by the power that granted them. Is that, in every instance, their whole nature? If it is not, we are apparently obliged to resort to the idea that a subject has certain inherent entitlements, liberties which he *ought* to have (not necessarily unconditionally), whether granted or no. We could then meaningfully say that some civic rights were rights before they became civic, and that we have other rights which ought to be made civic; in other words, that there are rights that are not wholly created by the ruling power, which can at most only acknowledge and

protect them. Now a right conceived as an inherent entitlement cannot mean something which we demand simply because we desire it strongly, for such a demand is only a natural fact. What it does mean is hard to state, perhaps because entitlement may be an ultimate idea. One old way of expressing it is that a right is what reason detects to be an appropriate or binding claim when men are regarded in their peculiarly human aspects; another is that every human individual has an "intrinsic value", which entitles him, regardless of his achievements, to respect; another is Kant's principle that each man is an end in himself, and is therefore not to be used as a mere tool. In the language of political philosophy, no man is to be treated as *only* a subject, as *wholly* under political authority and force — this being one of Spinoza's theses, not always obvious in his pedantic idiom.

Instead, however, of proceeding to deduce the specific rights, he narrows his argument to a claim for freedom of thought, of its utterance in speech and print, and makes the claim almost entirely for "philosophers", a term that in his day covered scientists as well as metaphysicians. Can we endorse his reasons? He says, as Plato and Aristotle had said, that "philosophical" thinking is man's highest activity. Nowadays we should want to argue the prior question whether human activities can be ranged in a single linear value-scale. He says it is the highest because its object is the highest conceivable, namely God[1]. We should hesitate to make its merit depend wholly on a religious presupposition. He meets "philosophers" on common ground when he notes, first, that expert intellectual activity is evidently a virtue (in the old double sense of vigour and excellence of mind); secondly, that its ineluctable aim is theoretical (though applicable) truth; and

---

[1] Spinoza was deeply religious. In his phrase "God or Nature" the second term does not mean the totality of observable fact (see Ep. 21, below, p. 129). This totality is in God, but is not the whole of Him. Hence, on the one hand, the more we know of it, the more we know of Him; on the other hand, complete discursive knowledge of it would be only one clue to His infinite nature. Spinoza's system was influenced by Neoplatonism, and stands near to this. To treat it as an episode in the history of Cartesianism is superficial.

thirdly, that it is autonomous, *i.e.* can be conducted only by the methods and criteria which that aim prescribes. A State that tries either to force or beguile a man capable of it into being disloyal to it is trampling on thinking in its austerest form. The case is, then, not that " philosophers" *want* to be free, but that they *must* be free *if* science and philosophy are to be pursued; and that a State that will not let them be free is both denying them the right to unfold their mental powers, and denying itself the varied benefits, spiritual and material, which only such men can provide.

Yet if they are to be free to teach and publish their questionings and conclusions openly, not furtively or behind closed doors, do they not then, stepping out into society, become subject to social and political norms? Surely they have no more right than other men to live in a State entirely on their own terms. Unless the right of open utterance can be proved to be absolute, it can be claimed only so far as it is compatible with the rights of other subjects, and with the rights of rulers who are required to keep peace and order. Here we touch the nerve of the political problem. Spinoza's text will not allow us to ignore it. The principle must, however, be interpreted fairly. For example, let us grant that " philosophers" should not scandalise their fellow-citizens; but in fact many people, of narrow orthodoxy or touchy in temperament, are all too easily scandalised. Let us grant that philosophers cannot be allowed to incite to political disobedience; yet quietly and honestly argued criticism of a law or constitution can be judged by proud or nervous rulers to be seditious, and can in fact, without intention, incite some people to sedition.

Rulers and the populace are imperfect. Let us admit that so too are " philosophers". Spinoza's portrait of them is somewhat idealised. They are not, he says, dangerous men, for they speak and write primarily to one another with moderation and respect, simply out of a common desire for truth, and they are unintelligible to the vast majority of the people. On the first point we must confess that higher learning, even natural science, is not free from acrimonious disputes, personal clashes, the pressing of prejudices as proved truths, and desire for fame and a following. The second point is scarcely tenable

at a time when organs of publicity can transmit the doubts, negations and affirmations of thinkers to a whole nation, not all the citizens of which are humble or brave enough to read or listen in order to learn.

The problem remains. Rulers must rule, and thinkers must think, confer and publish. The former have an urgent duty, the latter an unhurried one. The two duties, on a short view, are not always harmonious. Still, it is evident that if rulers, or in democracies their people, want to have the benefits of "philosophy" — in technical results and in the beckoning example of clear, ordered, disinterested and long-range thinking — they must leave their competent intellectuals free, for in this sphere at least "truth will out" holds only under that condition; and the open communication they must have among themselves will make it possible for their fellow-citizens to "listen in", unless these are controlled by watchdogs, as if they were sheep, instead of being governed as men. Milton spoke for the thinkers when he wrote, "The State shall be my governors, but not my critics", and for the readers when he found it a deep affront "that another should enjoin us to know nothing but by statute".

The problem is not, unfortunately, a merely academic one. There are still countries in which a religious orthodoxy can shackle speech and writing. There are countries in which intellectuals are subjected to a secular political orthodoxy. There are countries in which one school of philosophers almost silences other schools by controlling the learned societies, reviewing, and what students are recommended to read. And there are newly liberated countries whose leaders are easing their difficult task by trampling on intellectual critics as heavily as on rebels. One tragic proof is the number of intellectual refugees scattered about the world to-day, and the number rotting in prisons. There is room for orthodoxies; but when they are of the kind that *requires* intolerance, they cannot help offending reason, conscience and charity. When they are not of that kind, but are forced into intolerance by the need to control ignorant and hot-blooded masses — cases of necessity must be admitted — they can prove their innocence by seizing every chance of lightening the heavy hand. The *ideal* of

freedom cannot be discarded without continuing abasement. Nor can its kinds and degrees be realised at one stroke: which can be given and when, is to be determined not theoretically but by a political insight that sees human possibilities as well as human actualities. As Lord Acton said, liberty " is the delicate fruit of a mature civilisation ".

BIBLIOGRAPHICAL NOTE

The best collected editions of Spinoza's works in the original are those edited by J. van Vloten and J. P. N. Land (1882, 2 vols., The Hague; repr. 1895, 3 vols., and 1914, 4 vols.) and by C. Gebhardt for the Heidelberg Academy (1924, 4 vols.). There was an English translation of the works by R. H. M. Elwes, 1883-4, 2 vols., London. The *Tr. Pol.* had been translated separately by W. Maccall, 1854, London; and the *Tr. Theol.-Pol.* by R. Willis, 1862, London; the most competent edition is *The Political Works. The Tr. Theol.-Pol. in Part and the Tr. Pol. in Full*, edited and translated with introduction and notes by A. G. Wernham, 1958, Oxford. On the background R. H. Bainton's *Sebastian Castellio and the Toleration Controversy*, 1931, may be consulted, also J. W. Allen's *History of Political Thought in the Sixteenth Century*, 1928 (repr. 1960), London. In the histories of political philosophy Spinoza is given scant attention. In most books on Spinoza his political philosophy is not much considered: the only detailed study of it in English is *Spinoza's Political and Ethical Philosophy* by R. A. Duff, 1903, Glasgow. The most useful general study is probably *Spinoza, his Life and Philosophy*, by the jurist Sir Frederick Pollock, 2nd ed., 1899, London.

TRACTATUS THEOLOGICO-POLITICUS

continens dissertationes aliquot
quibus ostenditur libertatem philosophandi
non tantum salva pietate & reipublicae pace posse concedi
sed eandem nisi cum pace reipublicae ipsaque pietate
tolli non posse.

A THEOLOGICO-POLITICAL TREATISE

containing certain dissertations
in which it is argued that
freedom in philosophising can be granted
without hurt to religion and to the peace of the State,
and cannot be abolished without abolishing along with it
the peace of the State and religion itself.

PRAEFATIO

10. Verum enimvero si regiminis monarchici summum sit arcanum, eiusque omnino intersit homines deceptos habere et metum quo retineri debent specioso religionis nomine adumbrare, ut pro servitio tamquam pro salute pugnent, & ne turpe sed maximum decus esse putent in unius hominis iactationem sanguinem animamque impendere, nihil contra in libera republica excogitari, nec infelicius temptari potest, quando quidem communi libertati omnino repugnat, liberum uniuscuiusque iudicium praeiudiciis occupare vel aliquo modo coercere. **11.** Et quod ad seditiones attinet quae specie religionis concitantur, eae profecto inde tantum oriuntur quod leges de rebus speculativis conduntur & quod opiniones tamquam scelera pro crimine habentur & damnantur, quarum defensores & adseculae non publicae saluti sed odio ac saevitiae adversariorum tantum immolantur. Quod si ex iure imperii non nisi facta arguerentur & dicta impune essent, nulla iuris specie similes seditiones ornari possent nec controversiae in seditiones verterentur. **12.** Cum itaque nobis haec rara felicitas contigerit ut in republica vivamus * ubi unicuique iudicandi libertas integra & Deum ex suo ingenio colere conceditur, & ubi nihil libertate carius nec dulcius habetur, me rem non ingratam neque inutilem facturum credidi si ostenderem hanc libertatem non tantum salva pietate & reipublicae pace concedi, sed insuper eandem non nisi cum ipsa pace reipublicae ac pietate

---

* Amsterdam. See Ch. **XX**, sec. 40 (p. 82).

PREFACE

10. If in a monarchy the chief secret and concern be to keep men under deceit, and to spread the mantle of religion round the fear by which they have to be restrained, so that they may fight for slavery as if it were safety and think it not disgraceful but the greatest honour to give their lives for the glory of a single person; in a free State nothing more unsuitable than that could be contrived or undertaken, since it is altogether contrary to the general freedom to distort with prejudice, or coerce in any other way, the judgment of individuals. 11. The public revolts that are stirred up in the name of religion arise only when laws are made about matters of theoretical speculation and opinions are regarded as wicked and therefore condemned as crimes, the persons who hold or defend them being sacrificed not to the welfare of the State but only to the hate and rage of their adversaries. If the law forbade nothing but actions, leaving speech untouched, such uprisings could be given no legal colouring, and controversies would not pass into public disorder. 12. Now since I happen to have the unusual good fortune to live in a State * where each man is allowed complete freedom of thought and religion, and where nothing is regarded as more precious and enjoyable than freedom, I think it may not be unwelcome or fruitless to set forth arguments for the thesis that such freedom can be granted without hurt to religion and to the peace of the State, and cannot be abolished without at the same time

tolli posse. 13. Atque hoc praecipuum est quod in hoc tractatu demonstrare constitui....

20. Cum haec ergo animo perpenderem, scilicet lumen naturale non tantum contemni sed a multis tamquam impietatis fontem damnari, humana deinde commenta pro divinis documentis haberi, credulitatem fidem aestimari, et controversias philosophorum in ecclesia et in curia summis animorum motibus agitari, atque inde saevissima odia ac dissidia quibus homines facile in seditiones vertuntur, plurimaque alia quae hic narrare nimis longum foret, oriri animadverterem, sedulo statui Scripturam de novo integro et libero animo examinare et nihil de eadem adfirmare nihilque tamquam eius doctrinam admittere quod ab eadem clarissime non edocerer. 24. Sed cum in iis quae Scriptura expresse docet nihil reperissem quod cum intellectu non conveniret nec quod eidem repugnaret, & praeterea viderem Prophetas nihil docuisse nisi res admodum simplices quae ab unoquoque facile percipi poterant, atque has eo stylo adornavisse iisque rationibus confirmavisse quibus maxime multitudinis animus ad devotionem erga Deum moveri posset, omnino mihi persuasi Scripturam rationem absolute liberam relinquere et nihil cum philosophia commune habere, sed tam hanc quam illam proprio suo talo niti. 27. Fundamentalibus deinde fidei ostensis concludo denique obiectum cognitionis revelatae nihil esse praeter oboedientiam atque adeo a naturali cognitione tam obiecto quam fundamentis & mediis prorsus distinctam esse & nihil cum hac commune habere, sed tam hanc quam illam suum regnum absque ulla alterius repugnantia obtinere et neutram alterutri ancillari debere.

28. Porro quia hominum ingenium varium admodum est, & alius his alius illis opinionibus melius acquiescit & quod hunc ad religionem illum ad risum movet, inde cum supra dictis concludo unicuique sui iudicii libertatem & potestatem fundamenta fidei ex suo ingenio interpretandi relinquendam, & fidem uniuscuiusque ex solis operibus iudicandam num pia an impia sit. Sic ergo omnes integro & libero animo Deo oboe-

abolishing these. 13. To prove this is the main purpose of the present treatise....

20. As I thought over such matters as these—that natural reason is not only despised but also by many condemned as a source of impiety, that human imaginings are taken as divine teachings, that credulity is counted as faith, that the controversies of philosophers are passionately bandied about in Church and Court, rousing fierce hatreds and disagreements which easily pass into open factions, and other such matters too many to be mentioned here; as I thought over these, I determined to examine Scripture afresh, with an open and honest mind, and to make only such statements about it, and admit only so much as its teaching, as I could quite clearly learn from it itself. 24. In what Scripture teaches expressly I found nothing that is at variance with the intellect. I saw also that the Prophets taught nothing but very simple matters, which anybody could easily understand, and that they expressed those matters in such language, and supported them with such reasons, as would best move the hearts of the common people to devotion to God. I therefore became fully convinced that Scripture leaves reason entirely free, and has nothing in common with philosophy, each being left standing on its own feet. 27. When I have stated the basic articles of faith, I shall infer that revealed knowledge has as its aim simply obedience, and therefore is entirely distinct from natural knowledge, differing in aim, grounds, and means, the two having nothing in common, each ruling in its own domain without conflicting with the other, and neither being the servant of the other.

28. Further, the minds of men being very different—one man being prone to one set of opinions, another to another, and what moves one man to a religious attitude moving another to ridicule—I shall conclude from this, as well as from the preceding considerations, that each man should be left free to interpret the grounds of faith in his own way, and that his faith should be judged, as to its piety or impiety, entirely from his conduct; for then everybody would be able

dire poterunt, & sola iustitia et caritas apud omnes in pretio erit.

29. Postquam his libertatem quam lex divina revelata unicuique concedit ostendi, ad alteram quaestionis partem pergo, nempe hanc eandem libertatem salva reipublicae pace & summarum potestatum iure posse & etiam concedi debere, nec posse adimi absque magno pacis periculo magnoque totius reipublicae detrimento. Ad haec autem demonstrandum a iure naturali uniuscuiusque incipio, quod scilicet eo usque se extendit quo uniuscuiusque cupiditas & potentia se extendit, & quod nemo iure naturae ex alterius ingenio vivere tenetur sed suae unusquisque libertatis vindex est. 30. Praeterea ostendo hoc iure neminem revera cedere nisi qui potestatem se defendendi in alium transfert, atque eum necessario hoc ius naturale absolute retinere in quem unusquisque ius suum ex proprio suo ingenio vivendi simul cum potestate sese defendendi transtulit; atque hic ostendo eos qui summum imperium tenent ius ad omnia quae possunt habere, solosque vindices iuris & libertatis esse, reliquos autem ex solo eorum decreto omnia agere debere.

31. Verum quoniam nemo potestate sua se defendendi ita se privare potest ut homo esse desinat, hinc concludo neminem iure suo naturali absolute privari posse, sed subditos quaedam quasi naturae iure retinere quae iis adimi non possunt sine magno imperii periculo, quaeque adeo ipsis vel tacite conceduntur vel ipsi expresse cum iis qui imperium tenent stipulantur... 32. Post haec ostendo eos qui summum imperium tenent non tantum iuris civilis sed etiam sacri vindices & interpretes esse eosque solos ius habere discernendi quid iustum quid iniustum quid pium & quid impium sit; & tandem concludo eosdem hoc ius optime retinere & imperium tuto conservare posse si modo unicuique & sentire quae velit & quae sentiat dicere concedatur.*

---

* From Tacitus, *Historiae*, I. i: "rara temporum felicitate, ubi sentire quae velis et quae sentias dicere licet".

to obey God with his whole mind, and only justice and love would enjoy public esteem.

29. After thus making clear the freedom allowed by divine law so far as this is revealed, I shall pass to the other part of the inquiry, to prove that that freedom *can* be granted without hurt to the peace of the State and the authority of the Sovereign Power, that it *ought* to be granted, and that it cannot be taken away without imperilling peace and damaging every part of the State's life. I shall begin the proof of these contentions with the natural right of each person, maintaining that this right extends as far as his desire and power extend, and that by it no man is obliged to live under the direction of another, but is himself the protector of his freedom. 30. I shall argue further that nobody can really relinquish that right unless he transfers his power of self-defence to someone else, and that his natural right then necessarily and absolutely remains with him to whom he has transferred both his right to live as he pleases and his power of defending himself. From this I shall argue that rulers have the right to everything they have the actual power to do, and are the sole guardians of justice and freedom, by their decree alone all other men being bound in all their actions.

31. Since, however, no man can so far relinquish the power of defending himself as to cease to be a human being, I shall conclude that nobody can be deprived of his natural right absolutely, but that subjects retain, by something like natural right, certain powers which cannot be taken from them without great danger to the State, and which accordingly are either tacitly allowed to them or expressly stipulated by them in a contract with their rulers.... 32. I shall later argue that rulers are the guardians and interpreters of both civil and religious law, they alone having the right to pronounce what is just and what unjust, what pious and what impious. Finally, I shall conclude that rulers are best able to hold that right and to preserve the State only if they allow each man to think what he wills and say what he thinks.*

CAP. III

12. Omnia quae honeste cupimus ad haec tria potissimum referuntur, nempe res per primas suas causas intellegere, passiones domare sive virtutis habitum acquirere, et denique secure & sano corpore vivere. Media quae ad primum & secundum directe inserviunt & quae tamquam causae proximae & efficientes considerari possunt in ipsa humana natura continentur, ita ut eorum acquisitio a sola nostra potentia sive a solis humanae naturae legibus praecipue pendeat; & hac de causa omnino statuendum est haec dona nulli nationi peculiaria sed toti humano generi communia semper fuisse, nisi somniare velimus naturam olim diversa hominum genera procreavisse. 13. At media quae ad secure vivendum & corpus conservandum inserviunt in rebus externis praecipue sita sunt, atque ideo dona fortunae vocantur quia nimirum maxime a directione causarum externarum quam ignoramus pendent, ita ut hac in re stultus fere aeque felix & infelix ac prudens sit. Attamen ad secure vivendum & iniurias aliorum hominum & etiam brutorum evitandum, humana directio & vigilantia multum iuvare potest. 14. Ad quod nullum certius medium ratio & experientia docuit quam societatem certis legibus formare certamque mundi plagam occupare & omnium vires ad unum quasi corpus nempe societatis redigere. Verum enimvero ad societatem formandam & conservandam ingenium & vigilantia non mediocris requiritur, & idcirco illa societas securior erit & magis constans minusque fortunae obnoxia quae maxime ab hominibus prudentibus & vigilantibus fundatur & dirigitur.

CAP. IV *

1. Legis nomen absolute sumptum significat id secundum quod unumquodque individuum, vel omnia vel aliquot eiusdem

---

* This chapter is a rough summary of the philosophy expounded in Spinoza's chief work, *Ethics*.

CH. III. THE CONDITIONS OF HUMAN SECURITY

12. Everything that we can rightly desire may be brought under three heads—the understanding of things by their final causes, the taming of the passions or the acquiring of habitual virtue, and safety and health. The proximate and efficient causes of the first two lie within human nature itself, so that the attainment of them depends chiefly on our own power, i.e. on the laws of human nature. For this reason we must assume that those boons have not been peculiar to any one nation but have always been common to the whole human race, unless we lightly imagine that once upon a time Nature made very different kinds of men. **13.** The conditions of survival and safety, on the other hand, lie chiefly outside us, and are therefore called gifts of fortune, their causes being under a control of which we are ignorant; so that in this sphere of consideration the foolish and the sagacious are almost equally happy or unhappy. Nevertheless, in respect of security against our fellow-men, and against brute animals too, human control and vigilance can be of much use. **14.** Reason and experience teach us that there is no surer means to that end than to found a society having determinate laws, occupying a definite piece of territory, and uniting the strength of all the inhabitants into, so to speak, a single body, i.e. a genuinely social unity. As, however, the founding and maintaining of such a social unity calls for a high degree of intelligence and vigilance, that society will be safer, more stable, and less exposed to the mischances of fortune, in whose foundation and rule the chief part is played by men that are sagacious and vigilant.

CH. IV. THE DISTINCTION OF HUMAN AND DIVINE LAW *

1. The term "law" taken in its most general sense means the principle according to which each thing (either all or some

speciei, una eademque certa ac determinata ratione agunt, ea vero vel a necessitate naturae vel ab hominum placito dependet. Lex quae a necessitate naturae dependet illa est quae ex ipsa rei natura sive definitione necessario sequitur; ab hominum placito autem & quae magis proprie ius appellatur est ea quam homines ad tutius & commodius vivendum vel ob alias causas sibi & aliis praescribunt.... 5. Verum enimvero quoniam nomen legis per translationem ad res naturales applicatum videtur, & communiter per legem nihil aliud intellegitur quam mandatum quod homines & perficere & neglegere possunt... ideo lex particularius definienda videtur, nempe quod sit ratio vivendi quam homo sibi vel aliis ob aliquem finem praescribit. 6. Attamen quoniam verus finis legum paucis tantum patere solet & perplurimum homines ad eum percipiendum fere inepti sunt & nihil minus quam ex ratione vivunt, ideo legislatores, ut omnes aeque constringerent, alium finem longe diversum ab eo qui ex legum natura necessario sequitur sapienter statuerunt, nempe legum propugnatoribus promittendo id quod vulgus maxime amat, & contra iis qui eas violarent minitando id quod maxime timet; sicque conati sunt vulgum tamquam equum freno quoad eius fieri potest cohibere. 7. Unde factum est ut pro lege maxime haberetur ratio vivendi quae hominibus ex aliorum imperio praescribitur, & consequenter ut ii qui legibus obtemperant sub lege vivere dicantur & servire videantur; & revera qui unicuique suum tribuit quia patibulum timet is ex alterius imperio & malo coactus agit nec iustus vocari potest; at is qui unicuique suum tribuit ex eo quod veram legum rationem & earum necessitatem novit, is animo constanti agit & ex proprio non vero alieno decreto, adeoque iustus merito vocatur.

9. Cum itaque lex nihil aliud sit quam ratio vivendi quam homines ob aliquem finem sibi vel aliis praescribunt, ideo lex distinguenda videtur in humanam & divinam. Per humanam intellego rationem vivendi quae ad tutandam vitam & rempublicam tantum inservit; per divinam autem, quae solum summum bonum, hoc est, Dei veram cognitionem & amorem spec-

of the same species) acts in a regular and determinate way, either by a necessity of nature or by human decision. A law that depends on a necessity of nature is one that follows necessarily from the very nature or definition of a thing. One that depends on human decision, and which is more properly called an ordinance, is a law that men prescribe to themselves and others for the attaining of safety, amenity, or other ends....
5. Since the term " law " seems to be applied to natural things metaphorically, being used in common speech for a command, which men may in fact either carry out or ignore...it may be more closely defined as a rule of life which a man prescribes for himself or others for some goal. **6.** Now as the real goal of laws is evident to very few men, the great majority being scarcely fitted to perceive it and never living by reason, legislators, in order to put all alike under the same restraints, have wisely adopted a goal very different from that which follows from the nature of law: they promise those who respect the laws those things which the generality of men most like, and threaten those who disobey with those things which they most fear, trying thereby to restrain the masses (so far as this is possible) as a rider bridles his horse. **7.** Hence law is chiefly regarded as a rule of life imposed by those who have command over men, so that those who obey it are said to live *under* it, and seem to be in servitude; and it is indeed true that whoever gives a man his due only because he fears the scaffold is acting under the compulsion and threat of someone else, and cannot be called just. Anyone, however, who gives a man his due because he knows the real purpose and necessity of laws is acting with a firm mind, and by his own decision, not by another's, and is therefore called just rightly.

9. Law being, then, a rule of life which men for some end prescribe to themselves or others, it may be divided into two kinds, human and divine. By human law I mean a rule of life that has to do only with the safety of life and of the State. By divine law I mean one that concerns solely our supreme good, i.e. the true knowledge and love of God. I call

tat. Ratio cur hanc legem voco divinam est propter summi boni naturam, quam hic paucis & quam clare potero iam ostendam.

10. Cum melior pars nostri sit intellectus, certum est si nostrum utile revera quaerere velimus nos supra omnia debere conari ut eum quantum fieri potest perficiamus; in eius enim perfectione summum nostrum bonum consistere debet. Porro quoniam omnis nostra cognitio & certitudo quae revera omne dubium tollit a sola Dei cognitione dependet, tum quia sine Deo nihil esse neque concipi potest, tum etiam quia de omnibus dubitare possumus quam diu Dei nullam claram & distinctam habemus ideam, hinc sequitur summum nostrum bonum & perfectionem a sola Dei cognitione pendere &c. 11. Deinde cum nihil sine Deo nec esse nec concipi possit, certum est omnia quae in natura sunt Dei conceptum pro ratione suae essentiae suaeque perfectionis involvere atque exprimere, ac proinde nos quo magis res naturales cognoscimus eo maiorem & perfectiorem Dei cognitionem acquirere.... 12. Atque adeo tota nostra cognitio, hoc est summum nostrum bonum, non tantum a Dei cognitione dependet sed in eadem omnino consistit; quod etiam ex hoc sequitur quod homo pro natura & perfectione rei quam prae reliquis amat eo etiam perfectior est, & contra. Adeoque ille necessario perfectissimus est & de summa beatitudine maxime participat qui Dei, entis nimirum perfectissimi, intellectualem cognitionem supra omnia amat, eademque maxime delectatur... 13. Media igitur quae hic finis omnium humanarum actionum, nempe ipse Deus quatenus eius idea in nobis est, exigit, iussa Dei vocari possunt, quia quasi ab ipso Deo quatenus in nostra mente exsistit nobis praescribuntur, atque adeo ratio vivendi quae hunc finem spectat lex divina optime vocatur....

14. Cum itaque amor Dei summa hominis felicitas sit & beatitudo & finis ultimus & scopus omnium humanarum actionum, sequitur eum tantum legem divinam sequi qui Deum amare curat non ex timore supplicii neque prae amore alterius rei ut deliciarum famae &c., sed ex eo solo quod Deum

it divine because of the nature of the supreme good, which I shall now expound as clearly as brevity allows.

10. The best part of us being our intellect, we ought above everything else, if we really wish to seek what is beneficial to us, to do our utmost to perfect it, for in its perfection our supreme good must consist. Now all our knowledge, and the certainty that removes all doubt, depend solely on the knowledge of God, both because without God nothing can either exist or be conceived, and because we can have doubt about everything as long as we have no clear and distinct idea of God. It follows that our supreme good or perfection depends exclusively on the knowledge of God. 11. Now since nothing can exist or be conceived without God, all natural things include and express the concept of God in proportion to the fulness of content and the perfection of each, and therefore the more we learn about natural things the more and better do we come to know God.... 12. Consequently, all our knowledge, i.e. our supreme good, does not merely depend on the knowledge of God but entirely consists in this. This consequence follows also from the truth that the higher the nature and perfection of that which a man loves above all else, the better is the man himself; so that that man is necessarily the most perfect, and has the greatest share of the highest blessedness, who loves more than anything else the intellectual knowledge of God (since He is the most perfect Being) and finds therein his chief joy.... 13. The means requisite to this goal of human action (God so far as we possess the idea of Him) may be called the commands of God, because they are, as it were, prescribed to us by God Himself so far as He is in our minds; and the rule of life which has that goal in view is most appropriately called the divine law....

14. The love of God being man's highest felicity and blessedness and the ultimate goal of all human actions, only he is following the divine law whose concern it is to love God not through fear of punishment or through love of anything other than God (e.g. pleasure, fame, etc.), but solely because

novit, sive quod novit Dei cognitionem & amorem summum esse bonum... 16. Homo tamen carnalis haec intellegere nequit & ipsi vana videntur quia nimis ieiunam Dei habet cognitionem, & etiam quia in hoc summo bono nihil repperit quod palpet comedat aut denique quod carnem qua maxime delectatur adficiat, utpote quod in sola speculatione & pura mente consistit.

18. Si iam ad naturam legis divinae naturalis ut eam modo explicuimus attendamus, videbimus I. eam esse universalem sive omnibus hominibus communem, eam enim ex universali humana natura deduximus; II. eam non exigere fidem historiarum quaecumque demum eae fuerint, nam quando quidem haec lex divina naturalis ex sola consideratione humanae naturae intellegatur, certum est nos eam aeque concipere posse in Adamo ac alio quocumque homine, aeque in homine qui inter homines vivit ac in homine qui solitariam vitam agit. 19. Nec fides historiarum quantumvis certa Dei cognitionem & consequenter nec etiam Dei amorem nobis dare potest; amor enim Dei ab eius cognitione oritur, eius autem cognitio ex communibus notionibus per se certis & notis hauriri debet... Attamen... earum tamen lectionem ratione vitae civilis perutilem esse non negamus; quo enim hominum mores & condiciones quae ex nulla re melius quam ex eorum actionibus nosci possunt observaverimus & melius noverimus, eo inter ipsos cautius vivere nostrasque actiones & vitam eorum ingenio, quantum ratio fert, melius accommodare poterimus. 20. Videmus III. hanc legem divinam naturalem non exigere caerimonias, hoc est actiones quae in se indifferentes sunt & solo instituto bonae vocantur, vel quae aliquod bonum ad salutem necessarium repraesentant, vel si mavis actiones quarum ratio captum humanum superat; nihil enim lumen naturale exigit quod ipsum lumen non attingit, sed id tantum quod nobis clarissime indicare potest bonum sive medium ad nostram beatitudinem esse.... 21. IV. Denique videmus summum legis divinae praemium esse ipsam legem, nempe Deum cognoscere,

he knows God, in other words knows that the knowledge and love of God are the supreme good.... 16. The carnal man, on the other hand, cannot understand these things: they seem nothing to him because his knowledge of God is very scanty, and because in that supreme good (this being a purely spiritual activity) he finds nothing that feeds or pampers or in any other way appeals to his body, in which he finds his chief delight.

18. If now we scrutinise the nature of the divine law of nature as so expounded, four points will become evident. I. That it is universal, common to all men; for I have deduced it from human nature in general. II. That it does not require belief in any historical accounts whatever; for, the divine law of nature being known by simply considering human nature in its generality, it can be thought of as present in Adam as in any other man, and in men in society as in men who live alone. 19. Nor can belief, however certain, in anything historical give us the knowledge of God or the love or Him; for the love of God springs from the knowledge of Him, and this knowledge has to be drawn from the very general truths that are known directly and are directly certain.... I do not deny, however...that the reading of historical accounts can be very useful for life in a State, since the more we observe and understand the manners and circumstances of men, which are better known from their actions than from anything else, the more prudently can we live among them and adjust our actions and life, as far as reason allows, to their habits of mind. 20. III. That this divine law of nature requires no ceremonies, i.e. actions that are in themselves indifferent, being called good only by tradition, either as symbolising some good necessary for salvation or (if you prefer this way of putting it) as exceeding human comprehension. The natural light of reason does not demand anything beyond its own reach, but only what it can quite clearly point out to us as good or as a means to our blessedness.... 21. IV. That the supreme reward of the divine law is the law itself, i.e. knowing God and loving Him

eumque ex vera libertate & animo integro & constante amare, poenam autem horum privationem & carnis servitutem, sive animum inconstantem & fluctuantem.

CAP. V

18. Societas non tantum ad secure ab hostibus vivendum sed etiam ad multarum rerum compendium faciendum perutilis est & maxime etiam necessaria, nam nisi homines invicem operam mutuam dare velint, ipsis & ars & tempus deficeret ad se, quoad eius fieri potest, sustentandum & conservandum. 19. Non enim omnes ad omnia aeque apti sunt nec unusquisque potis esset ad ea comparandum quibus solus maxime indiget. Vires & tempus, inquam, unicuique deficerent si solus deberet arare seminare metere molere coquere texere suere & alia perplurima ad vitam sustentandum efficere, ut iam taceam artes & scientias quae etiam ad perfectionem humanae naturae eiusque beatitudinem sunt summe necessariae. 20. Videmus enim eos qui barbare sine politia vivunt vitam miseram & paene brutalem agere, nec tamen pauca illa misera & impolita quae habent sine mutua opera, qualis qualis ea sit, sibi comparant.

Iam si homines a natura ita essent constituti ut nihil nisi id quod vera ratio indicat cuperent, nullis sane legibus indigeret societas sed absolute sufficeret homines vera documenta moralia docere ut sponte integro & liberali animo id quod vere utile est agerent. 21. Verum longe aliter cum humana natura constitutum est: omnes quidem suum utile quaerunt, at minime ex sanae rationis dictamine sed perplurimum ex sola libidine & animi adfectibus abrepti (qui nullam temporis futuri aliarumque rerum rationem habent) res appetunt utilesque iudicant. 22. Hinc fit ut nulla societas possit subsistere absque imperio & vi & consequenter legibus, quae hominum libidinem atque effrenatum impetum moderentur & cohibeant. Non tamen humana natura patitur absolute se cogi, &, ut Seneca

with genuine freedom and with a pure and stable mind; and that the punishment for not following it is the deprivation of these, and slavery to the flesh, i.e. a fickle and disturbed mind.

CH. V. CIVIL SOCIETY AND CIVIL OBEDIENCE

18. Society is of great use, indeed indispensable, not only for security against enemies but also for lightening many forms of labour, for if men were not ready to help one another they would lack both the skill and the time to do what could be done for their bodily maintenance and survival. 19. They are not all equally fitted for all tasks, and each singly is incapable of providing for even his most necessary requirements. No one would have either strength or time enough to do his own ploughing, sowing, reaping, grinding, cooking, weaving, stitching, and the very many other things needful for keeping him alive, to say nothing of the arts and sciences, which are needful for human perfection and blessedness. 20. Observation shows that in fact people who are below the level of civilisation, with no politically ordered society, live a wretched and almost animal life, and even they do not get such poor and crude things as they have without some degree of co-operation.

If men were so constituted by nature as to desire nothing but what reason points out, society would need no laws at all; with nothing more than a sound moral instruction, of their own accord and wholemindedly they would do what is genuinely good for them. 21. But human nature is by no means so constituted. Everybody seeks his private good, and in what he regards and desires as good he is scarcely ever ruled by sound reason but is mostly carried away by his appetites and passions, which take no account of the future or of anything else. 22. In consequence, no society can continue without government and force, and therefore without laws to temper and restrain appetite and raw impulse. Not that human nature will submit to complete compulsion: as Seneca the tragic poet says, "Nobody

Tragicus ait, violenta imperia nemo continuit diu, moderata durant. Quamdiu enim homines ex solo metu agunt tamdiu id quod maxime nolunt faciunt, nec rationem utilitatis & necessitatis rei agendae tenent, sed id tantum curant ne capitis aut supplicii rei sint scilicet. Immo non possunt malo aut damno imperatoris, quamvis cum suo magno etiam malo, non tamen laetari ipsique omnia mala non cupere & ubi poterunt ,adferre. Homines deinde nihil minus pati possunt quam suis aequalibus servire & ab iis regi. Denique nihil difficilius quam libertatem hominibus semel concessam iterum adimere.

23. Ex his sequitur primo quod vel tota societas, si fieri potest, collegialiter imperium tenere debet ut sic omnes sibi & nemo suo aequali servire teneatur, vel si pauci aut unus solus imperium teneat, is aliquid supra communem humanam naturam habere vel saltem summis viribus conari debet vulgo id persuadere. 24. Deinde leges in quocumque imperio ita institui debent ut homines non tam metu quam spe alicuius boni quod maxime cupiunt retineantur; hoc enim modo unusquisque cupide suum officium faciet. 25. Denique quoniam oboedientia in eo consistit quod aliquis mandata ex sola imperantis auctoritate exsequatur, hinc sequitur eandem in societate cuius imperium penes omnes est & leges ex communi consensu sanciuntur nullum locum habere, & sive in tali societate leges augeantur vel minuantur populum nihilo minus aeque liberum manere, quia non ex auctoritate alterius sed ex proprio suo consensu agit. At contra accidit ubi unus solus imperium absolute tenet, nam omnes ex sola auctoritate unius mandata imperii exsequuntur, adeoque, nisi ita ab initio educati fuerint ut ab ore imperantis pendeant, difficile is poterit ubi opus erit novas leges instituere & libertatem semel concessam populo adimere.

will bear violent rule long; only moderate rule lasts." As long as men are ruled by fear alone they will do what they most dislike, taking no account of the benefit or necessity of the action in question, but thinking only of avoiding death or other punishment. Indeed, they cannot help even exulting over any misfortune or hurt that may happen to their ruler, even if it brings with it evil to themselves; nay more, they cannot help wishing him evil, and bringing it on him when they can. Besides, men cannot bear to be under the dominion of their equals. Also, nothing is harder than to take away a liberty once granted.

23. From all which it follows, first, that Sovereignty should if possible lie in the society as a whole, all the members being thereby bound to obey only themselves, no individual being bound to obey his equal; or if it reside in only one man (or a few men), he should be in some respect above the common run of men, or at least do his utmost to persuade them that he is. 24. Secondly, under *any* form of rule laws should be so devised as to restrain men less by fear than by the hope of some good which they greatly desire; for then each man would do his duty eagerly. 25. Lastly, since obedience consists in carrying out commands simply on the authority of the ruler, it can have no place in a society where Sovereignty resides in all and the laws rest on common consent; for both in the institution of new laws and the abrogation of old ones the people there remain equally free, acting not on any authority external to themselves but by their own collective agreement. The position is the opposite where one man holds absolute rule; for, all men here obeying ordinances simply on the authority of a single ruler, it will be difficult for the latter, when need arises, to institute new laws or to take away any freedom already granted to the people, unless these have been trained from the outset to depend entirely on his pronouncements.

CAP. XIII

4. Sequitur Scripturae doctrinam non sublimes speculationes neque res philosophicas continere sed res tantum simplicissimas quae vel a quovis tardissimo possunt percipi. Non satis itaque mirari possum eorum... ingenia qui scilicet tam profunda in Scriptura vident mysteria ut nulla humana lingua possint explicari, & qui deinde in religionem tot res philosophicae speculationis introduxerunt ut ecclesia academia & religio scientia vel potius altercatio videatur. 5. Verum quid miror si homines qui lumen supranaturale habere iactant philosophis qui nihil praeter naturale habent nolint cognitione cedere? Id sane mirarer si quid novi quod solius esset speculationis docerent & quod olim apud gentiles philosophos non fuerit tritissimum (quos tamen caecutiise aiunt); nam si inquiras quaenam mysteria in Scriptura latere vident nihil profecto reperies praeter Aristotelis aut Platonis aut alterius similis commenta, quae saepe facilius possit quivis idiota somniare quam literatissimus ex Scriptura investigare. 6. Etenim absolute statuere nolumus ad doctrinam Scripturae nihil pertinere quod solius sit speculationis... sed hoc tantum volo, talia admodum pauca atque admodum simplicia esse. 7. Quaenam autem ea sint & qua ratione determinentur hic ostendere constitui, quod nobis iam facile erit postquam novimus Scripturae intentum non fuisse scientias docere; hinc enim facile iudicare possumus nihil praeter oboedientiam eandem ab hominibus exigere, solamque contumaciam non autem ignorantiam damnare. 8. Deinde quia oboedientia erga Deum in solo amore proximi consistit... hinc sequitur in Scriptura nullam aliam scientiam commendari quam quae omnibus hominibus necessaria est ut Deo secundum hoc praescriptum oboedire possint & qua ignorata homines necessario debent esse contumaces vel saltem sine disciplina oboedientiae; reliquas autem speculationes quae huc directe non

CH. XIII. SCRIPTURE NOT PHILOSOPHICAL

4. The doctrinal content of Scripture includes no lofty speculations, no philosophical propositions, but only matters so simple that even the most untrained mind can grasp them. I am therefore greatly surprised at the mentality of those... who find in Scripture mysteries too deep to be elucidated in any merely human language and then bring into religion so much philosophical speculation that they make the Church look like a university and religion like a science, or, rather, like a disputation. 5. Yet why should I be surprised if men who proudly claim a supernatural illumination refuse to yield in the sphere of knowledge to philosophers, who have nothing but their natural faculties? I should be surprised, however, if they taught anything new in pure philosophy, anything that was not a commonplace among those pagan philosophers of old whom they nevertheless accuse of blindness; and when we inquire what the mysteries are that lie hidden in Scripture we find only notions from Aristotle or Plato or some such thinker, which could be detected in Scripture by the most learned scholar with even less probability than they could crop up in the imagination of any untrained fellow. 6. I would not, however, say without qualification that the doctrinal content of Scripture has no properly philosophical bearings at all...but only that these are very few and very simple. 7. I shall indicate later what these are and how they may be marked off, which will be an easy task when we have seen that the aim of Scripture is not to teach theoretical knowledge, for then it becomes clear that all it demands of man is obedience, condemning only refractoriness, not ignorance. 8. Since obedience to God is nothing more nor less than love of one's neighbour... the only knowledge commended in Scripture is that which everybody needs in order to be able to obey God in the way required by that precept, and the ignorance of which is bound to leave men refractory, or at least without any instruction in obedience. The speculative matters that do not

tendunt, sive eae circa Dei sive circa rerum naturalium cognitionem versentur, Scripturam non tangere atque adeo a religione revelata separandas.

CAP. XIV

3. Sectarios tamen istos nolumus ea de causa impietatis accusare quod scilicet verba Scripturae suis opinionibus accommodant; sicuti enim olim ipsa captui vulgi accommodata fuit, sic etiam unicuique eandem suis opinionibus accommodare licet si videt se ea ratione Deo in iis quae iustitiam & caritatem spectant pleniore animi consensu oboedire posse. 4. Sed ideo eosdem accusamus quod hanc eandem libertatem reliquis nolunt concedere, sed omnes qui cum iisdem non sentiunt, quamquam honestissimi & verae virtuti obtemperantes sint, tamquam Dei hostes tamen persequuntur, & contra eos qui iis assentantur, quamvis impotentissimi animi sint, tamen tamquam Dei electos diligunt, quo nihil profecto scelestius & reipublicae magis perniciosum excogitari potest.

5. Ut igitur constet quousque ratione fidei uniuscuiusque libertas sentiendi quae vult se extendit, & quosnam, quamvis diversa sentientes, tamquam fideles tamen aspicere tenemur, fides eiusque fundamentalia determinanda sunt; quod quidem in hoc Capite facere constitui, simulque fidem a philosophia separare, quod totius operis praecipuum intentum fuit....

6. Diximus in superiori Capite intentum Scripturae esse tantum oboedientiam docere. Quod quidem nemo infitias ire potest. Quis enim non videt utrumque Testamentum nihil esse praeter oboedientiae disciplinam, nec aliud utrumque intendere quam quod homines ex vero animo obtemperent? 7. Nam... Moses non studuit Israëlitas ratione convincere, sed pacto iuramentis & beneficiis obligare, deinde populo legibus obtempe-

bear on this point, whether they concern the knowledge of God or the knowledge of natural things, are not relevant to Scripture, and are therefore to be kept apart from revealed religion.

CH. XIV. THE NATURE AND CONTENT OF FAITH

3. I would not charge the sectaries with impiety for adapting the sayings of Scripture to their own opinions, for as they were originally adapted to the understanding of ordinary people, so it is permissible now for each individual to adapt them to his own opinions, if he finds by so doing that, in matters requiring justice and charity, he can obey God with a greater unity of mind and heart. 4. But I do charge them with refusing to allow this freedom to others, and with persecuting as God's enemies those, however decent and virtuous, whose opinions differ from theirs, and with favouring as God's elect those, however weak in character, whose opinions agree with theirs. Nothing could be more wicked than that, or more ruinous to the State.

5. In order to determine how far, in matters of faith, freedom of individual opinion extends, and who are to be regarded as truly possessing faith, despite the difference of their opinions, we must define faith and its fundamental requirements, making this the subject of the present chapter; and at the same time distinguish faith from philosophy, the drawing of this distinction being the chief purpose of the entire treatise....

6. I said in the preceding chapter that the purpose of Scripture is nothing but obedience. This is incontrovertible: it is obvious that obedience alone, wholehearted, is the lesson and aim of both the Old Testament and the New. 7.... According to the former, Moses did not try to convince the Israelites by rational argument, but to bind them by a covenant, oaths, and the prospect of benefits. He commanded obedience to the

rare sub poena interminatus est & praemiis eundem ad id hortatus, quae omnia media non ad scientias sed ad solam oboedientiam sunt. 8. Evangelica autem doctrina nihil praeter simplicem fidem continet, nempe Deo credere eumque revereri, sive, quod idem est, Deo oboedire.... 9. Deinde quidnam unusquisque exsequi debeat ut Deo obsequatur, ipsa etiam Scriptura plurimis in locis quam clarissime docet, nempe totam legem in hoc solo consistere, in amore scilicet erga proximum; quare nemo etiam negare potest quod is qui ex Dei mandato proximum tamquam se ipsum diligit revera est oboediens & secundum legem beatus, & qui contra odio habet vel neglegit rebellis est & contumax. 10. Denique apud omnes in confesso est Scripturam non solis peritis sed omnibus cuiuscumque aetatis & generis hominibus scriptam & vulgatam fuisse. Atque ex his solis evidentissime sequitur nos ex Scripturae iussu nihil aliud teneri credere quam id quod ad hoc mandatum exsequendum absolute necessarium sit. Quare hoc ipsum mandatum unica est totius fidei catholicae norma, & per id solum omnia fidei dogmata quae scilicet unusquisque amplecti tenetur determinanda sunt.

13. Ut itaque rem totam ordine ostendam, a fidei definitione incipiam, quae ex hoc dato fundamento sic definiri debet, nempe quod nihil aliud sit quam de Deo talia sentire quibus ignoratis tollitur erga Deum oboedientia, & <quae>* hac oboedientia posita necessario ponuntur.... 14. Quae autem ex eadem sequuntur paucis iam ostendam. Videlicet I. fidem non per se sed tantum ratione oboedientiae salutiferam esse.... II. Sequitur quod is qui vere est oboediens necessario veram & salutiferam habet fidem. 16. Ex quibus iterum sequitur nos neminem iudicare posse fidelem aut infidelem esse nisi ex operibus: nempe, si opera bona sunt, quamvis dogmatibus ab aliis fidelibus dissentiat, fidelis tamen est, & contra si mala sunt, quamvis verbis conveniat, infidelis tamen est.... 20. Sequitur denique fidem non tam requirere vera quam pia dogmata, hoc est talia quae ani-

---

* Not in Spinoza's text.

laws under threat of punishment and promise of reward—which are inducements not to philosophy but to obedience. 8. In the Gospels the teaching is entirely about simple faith, i.e. believing in God and revering Him or, which is the same, obeying Him.... 9. What is to be done in order to obey God is made perfectly clear in many places of Scripture, namely, that the whole Jewish Law consists in loving one's neighbour. Accordingly, anyone who because of this command of God loves his neighbour as himself is obedient, and by the very terms of the Law blessed; and anyone who hates or neglects his neighbour is rebellious and unruly. 10. In short, as is generally acknowledged, Scripture was written and published not for the learned only but for all men, of whatever age and race. It is evident, then, that so far as Scripture is concerned we are under obligation to believe only what is indispensable for carrying out that command. That command is therefore the sole norm of the catholic faith; by it alone must be determined what each individual is obliged to accept as dogmas of the faith.

13. To expound the subject in due order, I shall begin with a definition of faith. On the ground of the purpose of Scripture as stated, faith consists entirely in those beliefs about God without which obedience to Him is impossible, and which, when obedience is admitted, are implied by this.... 14. The implications of the definition can be stated briefly. The first is that faith saves not in itself but because of the obedience it requires...; from which follows the second, that he who is truly obedient has of necessity a true and saving faith. 16. Hence we cannot judge whether anyone is a "believer" or an "unbeliever" except from his works: if these are good, he is a believer, however much he may differ in respect of dogmas from other believers, and if his works are bad, he is an unbeliever, however much he may agree in words with believers.... 20. I conclude that what faith requires is not so much true dogmas as pious ones, i.e. those that move the

mum ad oboedientiam movent, tametsi inter ea plurima sint quae nec umbram veritatis habent, dummodo tamen is qui eadem amplectitur eadem falsa esse ignoret, alias rebellis necessario esset. Quomodo enim fieri posset ut aliquis qui iustitiam amare & Deo obsequi studet tamquam divinum adoret quod a divina natura alienum scit esse? 21. At animi simplicitate errare possunt homines, & Scriptura non ignorantiam sed solam contumaciam, ut iam ostendimus, damnat....

22. Cum itaque uniuscuiusque fides ratione oboedientiae vel contumaciae tantum, & non ratione veritatis aut falsitatis, pia vel impia sit habenda, & nemo dubitet commune hominum ingenium varium admodum esse nec omnes in omnibus aeque acquiescere, sed opiniones diverso modo homines regere, quippe quae hunc devotionem eae ipsae alterum ad risum & contemptum movent, hinc sequitur ad fidem catholicam sive universalem nulla dogmata pertinere de quibus inter honestos potest dari controversia.

24. ... Nec iam verebor fidei universalis dogmata sive universae Scripturae intenti fundamentalia enumerare, quae (ut ex iis quae in his duobus Capitibus ostendimus evidentissime sequitur) omnia huc tendere debent, nempe dari ens supremum quod iustitiam et caritatem amat, cuique omnes ut salvi sint oboedire tenentur eumque cultu iustitiae & caritate erga proximum adorare, atque hinc facile omnia determinantur, quaeque adeo nulla praeter haec sunt. 25. Videlicet I. Deum, hoc est ens supremum, summe iustum & misericordem sive verae vitae exemplar, exsistere. Qui enim nescit vel non credit ipsum exsistere ei oboedire nequit neque eum iudicem noscere. II. Eum esse unicum. Hoc enim etiam ad supremam devotionem admirationem & amorem erga Deum absolute requiri nemo dubitare potest; devotio namque admiratio & amor ex sola excellentia unius supra reliquos orientur. 26. III. Eum ubique esse praesentem vel omnia ipsi patere. Si res ipsum latere crederentur vel ipsum omnia videre ignoraretur, de aequitate eius

mind to obedience—even if many of them be without a shadow of truth, so long as he who believes them is not aware of their falsity, since otherwise he would be, of course, a rebel, for how could anybody who tries to love justice and obey God worship as divine anything he knows to be alien to the divine nature? 21. Men can fall into error through simplemindedness; what Scripture condemns, however, is not ignorance but only insolence....

22. Since, then, each man's faith is to be regarded as pious or impious only so far as it involves obedience or intractableness, not so far as it is true or false; and since the minds of men vary considerably, not all being equally acquiescent in all matters, and not being affected by their opinions in the same way, so that the same opinion leads one man to worship and another to scoff and despise; it follows that no dogmas about which good men can honestly disagree are part of the catholic or universal faith.

24... I may now venture to list the dogmas of the universal faith, the basic lessons of Scripture as a whole, which (as should be perfectly evident from what has been argued in this chapter and the preceding one) amount to this, that there is a supreme Being, who loves justice and charity, whom all men, if they are to be saved, ought to obey, and that He is to be worshipped by the practice of justice and by love of one's neighbour. From that all the indispensable dogmas are easily derived. They are the following, and no more. 25. I. That God exists, meaning a supreme Being, perfectly just and merciful, i.e. the model of the true life. Whoever is not aware of His existence, or does not believe it, cannot obey Him or acknowledge Him as Judge. II. That He is unique. This belief is utterly requisite for the highest religious devotion, wonder, and love, for these attitudes are excited only by a being that excels all other beings. 26. III. That He is present everywhere; in other words, that all things are manifest to Him. If men believed that anything is hidden from Him, or were unaware that He sees everything, they would doubt the impartiality of the justice

iustitiae qua omnia dirigit dubitaretur vel ipsa ignoraretur. IV. Ipsum in omnia supremum habere ius & dominium, nec aliquid iure coactum sed ex absoluto beneplacito & singulari gratia facere. Omnes enim ipsi absolute oboedire tenentur ipse autem nemini. 27. V. Cultum Dei eiusque oboedientiam in sola iustitia & caritate sive amore erga proximum consistere. VI. Omnes qui hac vivendi ratione Deo oboediunt salvos tantum esse, reliquos autem qui sub imperio voluptatum vivunt perditos. Si homines hoc firmiter non crederent nihil causae esset cur Deo potius quam voluptatibus obtemperare mallent. 28. VII. Denique Deum paenitentibus peccata condonare. Nullum enim est qui non peccet; si igitur hoc non statueretur, omnes de sua salute desperarent....

29. Atque haec omnia nemo ignorare potest apprime cognitu necessaria esse ut homines nullo excepto ex praescripto legis supra explicato Deo oboedire possint, nam horum aliquo sublato tollitur etiam oboedientia. 30. Ceterum quid Deus, sive illud verae vitae exemplar sit, an scilicet sit ignis spiritus lux cogitatio &c., id nihil ad fidem, ut nec etiam qua ratione sit verae vitae exemplar, an scilicet propterea quod animum iustum & misericordem habet vel quia res omnes per ipsum sunt & agunt, & consequenter nos etiam per ipsum intellegimus & per ipsum id quod verum aequum & bonum est videmus; perinde est quicquid de his unusquisque statuerit. 31. Deinde nihil etiam ad fidem si quis credat quod Deus secundum essentiam vel secundum potentiam ubique sit, quod res dirigit ex libertate vel necessitate naturae, quod leges tamquam princeps praescribat vel tamquam aeternas veritates doceat, quod homo ex arbitrii libertate vel ex necessitate divini decreti Deo oboediat, quodque denique praemium bonorum & poena malorum naturalis vel supranaturalis sit. 32. Haec & similia, inquam, nihil refert in respectu fidei qua ratione unusquisque intellegat, dummodo nihil eum in finem concludat ut maiorem licentiam ad peccandum sumat vel ut minus

with which He rules all things, or else be wholly ignorant of it. IV. That He has supreme right and rule over all things, not doing anything under the constraint of a right belonging to any other being, but only at His good pleasure and by His unique grace; for while men are unconditionally subject to Him, He is under no obligation at all to anybody. 27. V. That the worship of God and obedience to Him consist wholly in justice and in charity or love towards one's neighbour. VI. That all who obey God in this rule of life are saved, and all others, who live under the dominion of pleasure, are ruined. If this were not firmly believed, there would be no motive for preferring to obey God rather than pleasure. 28. VII. Lastly, that God pardons the sins of those who repent. Without this doctrine, since all men sin, all men would have no hope of salvation....

29. All these doctrines must be known if all men whatever are to be capable of obeying God in accordance with the law explicated above, for if any of them be taken away the ground of obedience is destroyed. 30. But what God, the model of the true life, is, e.g. whether He be fire, breath, light, thought, or anything else, does not concern faith; neither does the question why He is the model of true living, e.g. whether it is because He is just and merciful, or because all things exist and act by means of Him, so that we understand things through Him, and through Him see what is true and just and good. On these matters let it be as each man may decide. 31. Nor does it concern faith whether anybody believes that God's omnipresence follows necessarily from His essence or from His power, whether He rules freely or by a necessity of His nature, whether He imposes laws as a monarch or conveys them to us as eternal truths, whether man obeys God with a free will or is necessitated by divine decree, or whether the reward of the good and the punishment of the wicked are natural or supernatural. 32. How each man works out such questions has nothing to do with faith, provided his motive for adopting any answer is not to give himself an excuse for

fiat Deo obtemperans; quin immo unusquisque, ut iam supra diximus, haec fidei dogmata ad suum captum accommodare tenetur eaque sibi eo modo interpretari quo sibi videtur eadem facilius sine ulla haesitatione sed integro animi consensu amplecti posse, ut consequenter Deo pleno animi consensu oboediat.

33. ... Ostendimus enim fidem non tam veritatem quam pietatem exigere & non nisi ratione oboedientiae piam & salutiferam esse; & consequenter neminem nisi ratione oboedientiae fidelem esse. Quare non ille qui optimas ostendit rationes optimam necessario ostendit fidem, sed ille qui optima ostendit opera iustitiae & caritatis. 34. Quae doctrina quam salutaris quamque necessaria sit in republica ut homines pacifice & concorditer vivant, quotque inquam quantasque perturbationum & scelerum causas praescindat, omnibus iudicandum relinquo.

37. Superest iam ut tandem ostendam inter fidem sive theologiam & philosophiam nullum esse commercium nullamve adfinitatem, quod iam nemo potest ignorare qui harum duarum facultatum & scopum & fundamentum novit, quae sane toto caelo discrepant. 38. Philosophiae enim scopus nihil est praeter veritatem; fidei autem, ut abunde ostendimus, nihil praeter oboedientiam & pietatem. Deinde philosophiae fundamenta notiones communes sunt, & ipsa ex sola natura peti debet; fidei autem historiae & lingua & ex sola Scriptura & revelatione petenda.... 39. Fides igitur summam unicuique libertatem ad philosophandum concedit, ut quicquid velit de rebus quibuscumque sine scelere sentire possit, & eos tantum tamquam haereticos & schismaticos damnat qui opiniones docent ad contumaciam odia contentiones & iram suadendum, & eos contra fideles tantum habet qui iustitiam & caritatem pro viribus suae rationis & facultatibus suadent.

CAP. XV

1. Qui philosophiam a theologia separare nesciunt disputant num Scriptura rationi an contra ratio Scripturae debeat

sinning more boldly or becoming less obedient to God. As I have already said, everyone is under an obligation to adjust the dogmas of faith to his own intellect, and understand them in the way that seems most natural to him, so that he may be able to embrace them unwaveringly and with his whole mind, and thus obey God with complete sincerity.

33... I have shown that what faith requires is not so much truth as piety, and that it is pious and saving only so far as it in fact produces obedience. It is not, then, he who gives the best arguments that necessarily has the best faith, but he who shows the best fruits of justice and love. 34. How beneficial and necessary this doctrine is in a State for internal peace and concord, and how many and what great roots of disturbance and wickedness it would cut out, I leave everybody to judge for himself.

37. What now remains to be stated is that between faith or theology and philosophy there is neither connection nor affinity, as no one can fail to see who knows the aims and bases of these two disciplines, which are poles apart. 38. The only aim of philosophy is truth; of faith, only obedience and piety. The bases of philosophy are very general self-evident truths, which are to be sought in nature alone; of faith, historically recorded events and discourses, which are to be sought in Scripture and revelation alone.... 39. Faith therefore allows every thinker entire freedom of philosophising, so that each man may hold guiltlessly whatever opinion he will about anything. It condemns as heretics and schismatics those only who teach opinions in order to lead men to defiance, hatred, anger and quarrelling; and it regards as believers those only who use their mental abilities to the utmost to lead men to justice and charity.

CH. XV. FAITH AND REASON EACH AUTONOMOUS

1. Those who do not see that philosophy and theology are distinct argue the question whether Scripture should be the

ancillari; hoc est, an sensus Scripturae rationi an vero ratio Scripturae accommodari debeat; atque hoc a scepticis qui rationis certitudinem negant, illud autem a dogmaticis defenditur. 2. Sed tam hos quam illos toto caelo errare ex iam dictis constat. Nam utram sequamur sententiam, vel rationem vel Scripturam corrumpere necesse est. Ostendimus enim Scripturam non res philosophicas sed solam pietatem docere, & omnia quae in eadem continentur ad captum & praeconceptas opiniones vulgi fuisse accommodata. 3. Qui igitur ipsam ad philosophiam accommodare vult is sane Prophetis multa quae ne per somnium cogitarunt adfinget & perperam eorum mentem interpretabitur. Qui autem contra rationem & philosophiam theologiae ancillam facit is antiqui vulgi praeiudicia tamquam res divinas tenetur admittere & iisdem mentem occupare & occaecare. Adeoque uterque, hic scilicet sine ratione ille vero cum ratione, insaniet.

26. Verum enimvero quando quidem theologiae fundamentum, quod scilicet homines vel sola oboedientia salvantur, ratione non possumus demonstrare verum sit an falsum, potest ergo nobis etiam obici cur igitur id credimus; si sine ratione tamquam caeci id ipsum amplectimur, ergo nos etiam stulte & sine iudicio agimus. 27. Quod si contra statuere velimus hoc fundamentum ratione demonstrari posse, erit ergo theologia philosophiae pars nec ab eadem esset separanda. Sed ad haec respondeo me absolute statuere hoc theologiae fundamentale dogma non posse lumine naturali investigari vel saltem neminem fuisse qui ipsum demonstraverit; & ideo revelationem maxime necessariam fuisse. At nihilo minus nos iudicio uti posse ut id iam revelatum morali saltem certitudine amplectamur. 28. Dico morali certitudine nam non est quod expectemus nos de eo certiores esse posse quam ipsos Prophetas, quibus primo revelatum fuit & quorum tamen certitudo non

servant of reason or reason the servant of Scripture, i.e. whether the meaning of Scripture should be adjusted to reason or reason to Scripture. The latter position is taken by the sceptics who deny the certainty of reason, the former by the philosophical dogmatists. 2. From what I have said earlier it should be clear that both parties are quite wrong, for if we adopt the first position we are bound to falsify Scripture, and if the second we are bound to falsify reason. I have proved that Scripture does not teach philosophical matters but only piety, and that its contents are all adjusted to the mentality and preconceptions of the generality of men. 3. Hence anyone who tries to adjust Scripture to philosophy will attribute to the Prophets many ideas which the Prophets never dreamed of, and so will interpret them very wrongly; and anyone who makes reason or philosophy the servant of theology will be bound to admit as divine the prejudices of an ancient people, and so clutter and blind his mind with these prejudices. In both cases alike we should be demented, in the latter without reason, in the former with it.

26. Since the basic doctrine of theology—that men are saved only by obedience—cannot be proved or disproved rationally, the objection may be raised, "Why, then, believe it? If we accept it irrationally, as if we were mentally blind, we are being foolish, using no judgment; 27. and if we hold that it can be rationally proved, we are making theology an inseparable part of philosophy." To this objection I reply that I have asserted without qualification that that basic doctrine of theology cannot be examined by the light of reason (at any rate, nobody has ever managed to give a rational proof of it), and must therefore be a revelation which mankind needs greatly. Nevertheless, although it be by revelation that it has come to us, we can bring our power of judgment to bear on it, with the result that we can accept it with at any rate moral certainty. 28. I say "moral" certainty because we cannot hope to be more certain of it than the Prophets were to whom it was originally revealed; and their certainty was only a moral

nisi moralis fuit.... **29.** Ii igitur tota errant via qui Scripturae auctoritatem mathematicis demonstrationibus ostendere conantur. Nam Bibliorum auctoritas ab auctoritate Prophetarum dependet, adeoque ipsa nullis fortioribus argumentis demonstrari potest quam iis quibus Prophetae olim suo populo persuadere solebant....

37. Nam inscitia quidem est id quod tot Prophetarum testimoniis confirmatum est & ex quo magnum solamen iis qui ratione non ita pollent oritur, & reipublicae non mediocris utilitas sequitur, & quod absolute sine periculo aut damno credere possumus, nolle tamen amplecti, idque ea sola de causa quia mathematice demonstrari nequit; quasi vero ad vitam sapienter instituendam nihil tamquam verum admittamus quod ulla dubitandi ratione in dubium revocari queat, aut quod pleraeque nostrae actiones non admodum incertae sint & alea plenae.

38. Equidem fateor, qui putant philosophiam & theologiam sibi invicem contradicere & propterea alterutram e suo regno deturbandam existimant & huic aut illi valedicendum, eos non absque ratione studere theologiae firma fundamenta iacere eamque mathematice demonstrare conari. Quis enim nisi desperatus & insanus rationi temere valedicere vellet, vel artes & scientias contemnere & rationis certitudinem negare? **39.** At interim eos absolute excusare non possumus quando quidem rationem in auxilium vocare volunt ad eandem repellendam & certa ratione eandem incertam reddere conantur. Immo dum student mathematicis demonstrationibus theologiae veritatem & auctoritatem ostendere & rationi & lumini naturali auctoritatem adimere, nihil aliud faciunt quam ipsam theologiam sub rationis imperium trahere & plane videntur supponere theologiae auctoritatem nullum habere splendorem nisi lumine naturali rationis illustretur.

44. Iam antequam ad alia pergam hic expresse monere volo (tametsi iam dictum sit) circa utilitatem & necessitatem Sacrae Scripturae sive revelationis, quod ipsam permagnam statuo. Nam quando quidem non possumus lumine naturali

one.... **29.** They are wholly wrong, then, who try to give strictly deductive proofs of the authority of Scripture, for this authority depends on the authority of the Prophets, and therefore cannot be given any stronger proofs than those which they habitually used to convince their own people....

37. It would certainly be crude to refuse to accept, simply on the ground that it cannot be proved deductively, that which is confirmed by the testimony of so many Prophets, which brings great comfort to those who are incapable of philosophical reasoning, has very beneficial consequences to the State, and can be believed without the slightest danger or hurt. That would be tantamount to supposing that for wise living we should admit nothing as true which could in any way be doubted, or that most of our actions are not very uncertain, little more than gambles.

38. I grant that those who suppose philosophy and theology to be mutually contradictory, and accordingly hold that one or the other of them must be pulled down from its throne or banished, are not unreasonable in seeking to lay firm foundations for theology by trying to set out its contents in a rigorously deductive form. Would anyone, except in despair or madness, dare to dismiss reason altogether, denying its certainty and despising the sciences and the useful arts? **39.** I cannot, however, altogether excuse them when they call in the help of reason to refute reason, relying on reasoning to prove that reasoning is unreliable; for while they are busying themselves to demonstrate by strict deduction the truth and authority of theology, and thereby to disprove the authority of the natural light of reason, they are really putting theology itself under the dominion of reason, obviously implying that it is from the natural light of reason that the authority of theology derives whatever lustre it may have.

44. Before I proceed to other matters I must expressly declare (although I have done so earlier) that I set a high value on the usefulness and necessity of Scripture or revelation; for as we are unable to see by the natural light of reason that

percipere quod simplex oboedientia via ad salutem sit, sed sola revelatio doceat id ex singulari Dei gratia quam ratione adsequi non possumus fieri, hinc sequitur Scripturam magnum admodum solamen mortalibus attulisse. 45. Quippe omnes absolute oboedire possunt, & non nisi paucissimi sunt si cum toto humano genere comparentur qui virtutis habitum ex solo rationis ductu acquirunt, adeoque nisi hoc Scripturae testimonium haberemus de omnium fere salute dubitaremus.

CAP. XVI

1. Huc usque philosophiam a theologia separare curavimus & libertatem philosophandi ostendere quam haec unicuique concedit. Quare tempus est ut inquiramus quousque haec libertas sentiendi & quae unusquisque sentit dicendi in optima republica se extendat. Hoc ut ordine examinemus, de fundamentis reipublicae disserendum, & prius de iure naturali uniuscuiusque, ad rempublicam & religionem nondum attendentes.

2. Per ius & institutum naturae nihil aliud intellego quam regulas naturae uniuscuiusque individui secundum quas unumquodque naturaliter determinatum concipimus ad certo modo exsistendum & operandum. Ex. gr. pisces a natura determinati sunt ad natandum, magni ad minores comedendum, adeoque pisces summo naturali iure aqua potiuntur & magni minores comedunt. 3. Nam certum est naturam absolute consideratam ius summum habere ad omnia quae potest, hoc est, ius naturae eo usque se extendere quousque eius potentia se extendit; naturae enim potentia ipsa Dei potentia est, qui summum ius ad omnia habet. 4. ... Et quia lex summa naturae est ut unaquaeque res in suo statu quantum in se est conetur perseverare, idque nulla alterius sed tantum sui habita ratione, hinc sequitur unumquodque individuum ius summum ad hoc habere, hoc est (uti dixi) ad exsistendum & operandum prout naturaliter determinatum est. 5. Nec hic ullam agnoscimus differentiam inter homines & reliqua naturae individua, neque inter homines

simple obedience is the way to salvation, and only by revelation learn that it is so because of the peculiar grace of God, which reason cannot grasp, Scripture has brought to mortals much consolation. 45. All men can certainly become obedient; but only a very small fraction of the race can become virtuous under the guidance of their reason alone, so that without the witness of Scripture we should doubt whether any but a very few could be saved.

CH. XVI. THE NATURAL BASIS OF THE STATE. THE RIGHT TO RULE AND THE POWER TO RULE

1. So far, we have been concerned to separate philosophy from theology, and to show that the separation allows everyone to philosophise freely. It is now time to inquire how far this freedom of thought, and of expression of thought as well, extends in the best kind of State. To proceed in due order, I must discuss the basic reasons of there being a State at all, and shall therefore begin with the natural right of the individual, deferring for the moment the consideration of the State itself and of religion.

2. By the right or ordinance of nature I mean the natural rules in accordance with which we conceive every individual thing to be naturally determined to exist and act in a definite way. For example, fishes are determined by nature to swim, and the larger ones to eat the smaller ones; they do so by an unquestionable natural right. 3. Obviously, nature considered in itself has a complete right to do everything of which it is capable, i.e. its right is co-extensive with its power; for the power of nature is the power of God, who has complete right to everything. 4... Now since the highest law of nature is that everything strives as much as it can to persist in its distinctive mode of being, without taking into account anything other than itself, every individual thing has complete right to exist and act as it is naturally determined to do. 5. There is no need in this respect to draw a distinction between human beings

ratione praeditos & inter alios qui veram rationem ignorant, neque inter fatuos, delirantes & sanos. Quicquid enim unaquaeque res ex legibus suae naturae agit id summo iure agit, nimirum quia agit prout ex natura determinata est nec aliud potest. 6. Quare inter homines, quamdiu sub imperio solius naturae vivere considerantur, tam ille qui rationem nondum novit vel qui virtutis habitum nondum habet, ex solis legibus appetitus summo iure vivit, quam ille qui ex legibus rationis vitam suam dirigit; hoc est, sicuti sapiens ius summum habet ad omnia quae ratio dictat sive ex legibus rationis vivendi, sic etiam ignarus & animi impotens summum ius habet ad omnia quae appetitus suadet sive ex legibus appetitus vivendi....

7. Ius itaque naturale uniuscuiusque hominis non sana ratione sed cupiditate & potentia determinatur. Non enim omnes naturaliter determinati sunt ad operandum secundum regulas & leges rationis, sed contra omnes ignari omnium rerum nascuntur, & antequam veram vivendi rationem noscere possunt & virtutis habitum acquirere, magna aetatis pars, etsi bene educati fuerint, transit, & nihilo minus interim vivere tenentur seque quantum in se est conservare, nempe ex solo appetitus impulsu, quando quidem natura iis nihil aliud dedit, & actualem potentiam ex sana ratione vivendi denegavit, & propterea non magis ex legibus sanae mentis vivere tenentur quam felis ex legibus naturae leoninae. 8. Quicquid itaque unusquisque qui sub solo naturae imperio consideratur sibi utile vel ductu sanae rationis vel ex adfectuum impetu iudicat, id summo naturae iure appetere, & quacumque ratione, sive vi sive dolo sive precibus sive quocumque demum modo facilius poterit, ipsi capere licet, & consequenter pro hoste habere eum qui impedire vult quominus animum expleat suum.

and other natural things, or between humans with a developed reason and those without, or between the foolish, the mad, and the sane. Whatever anything does by the law of its own nature, it does with the greatest right, for it is acting in the way which nature determined, and cannot do otherwise. 6. Hence among human beings too, so long as they are considered as living solely under the dominion of nature, those who have not yet acquired the use of reason or a disposition to virtue live by nothing but the laws of appetite with as complete a right as those who order their life by the laws of reason; i.e. just as the wise have a complete right to everything that reason dictates, i.e. to live by the laws of reason, so those who are ignorant and not masters of themselves have a complete right to everything that appetite urges, i.e. to live by the laws of appetite....

7. The natural right of each man is determined, then, not by sound reason but by desire and the power to fulfil desire. Not all men are naturally determined to act according to the rules or laws of reason. Indeed, all are born completely ignorant, and before they can come to know the true law of living or acquire a disposition to virtue, a considerable part of their life has to elapse, even if they have been reared well. In the meantime they have to go on living, preserving themselves as best they can, i.e. entirely by the force of appetite, nature having given them nothing else, thereby denying them the ability to live by sound reason, so that they can no more be obliged to live by the laws of this than a cat by the laws of a lion's nature. 8. Consequently, whatever any man, considered in so far as he is under the rule of nature only, judges to be beneficial to himself, whether under the guidance of sound reason or under the impulsion of his feelings, he seeks it by the commanding right of nature, and by the same right may get it by any means—force, fraud, entreaty, or whatever on each occasion he may find convenient—and therefore may treat as an enemy anyone who intends to prevent him from satisfying his desires.

10... Natura non legibus humanae rationis, quae non nisi hominum verum utile & conservationem intendunt, intercluditur, sed infinitis aliis quae totius naturae, cuius homo particula est, aeternum ordinem respiciunt, ex cuius sola necessitate omnia individua certo modo determinantur ad exsistendum & operandum. 11. Quicquid ergo nobis in natura ridiculum absurdum aut malum videtur, id inde venit quod res tantum ex parte novimus, totiusque naturae ordinem & cohaerentiam maxima ex parte ignoramus, & quod omnia ex usu nostrae rationis dirigi volumus, cum tamen id quod ratio malum esse dictat non malum sit respectu ordinis & legum universae naturae, sed tantum solius nostrae naturae legum respectu.

12. Verum enimvero quanto sit hominibus utilius secundum leges & certa nostrae rationis dictamina vivere quae, uti diximus, non nisi verum hominum utile intendunt, nemo potest dubitare. Praeterea nullus est qui non cupiat secure extra metum quoad fieri potest vivere, quod tamen minime potest contingere quamdiu unicuique ad libitum omnia facere licet, nec plus iuris rationi quam odio & irae conceditur. 13. Nam nullus est qui inter inimicitias odia iram & dolos non anxie vivat quaeque adeo quantum in se est non conetur vitare. Quod si etiam consideremus homines absque mutuo auxilio miserrime & absque rationis cultu necessario vivere, ut in Cap. V ostendimus, clarissime videbimus homines ad secure & optime vivendum necessario in unum conspirare debuisse, ac proinde effecisse ut ius quod unusquisque ex natura ad omnia habebat collective haberent, neque amplius ex vi & appetitu uniuscuiusque sed ex omnium simul potentia & voluntate determinaretur. 14. Quod tamen frustra tentassent si nisi quod appetitus suadet sequi vellent (ex legibus enim appetitus unusquisque diverse trahitur), adeoque firmissime statuere & pacisci debuerunt ex solo rationis dictamine (cui nemo aperte repugnare audet ne mente carere videatur) omnia dirigere, & appetitum quatenus in damnum alterius aliquid suadet frenare,

10.... Nature is not bounded by the laws of human reason, for these aim at the true benefit and survival of human beings only, but by very many other laws, which have in view the eternal order of nature in its entirety, of which man is but a very small part; and by the necessity of this order alone everything whatever is determined to exist and act in a definite way. 11. Therefore whatever in nature seems to us to be senseless, absurd or evil seems so because we know things only in part, being almost entirely ignorant of the order and coherence of nature as a whole, and because we want everything to be ruled as our reason would rule. What reason pronounces to be evil is so only by the laws of *our* nature, not by the order and laws of nature as a whole.

12. Still, it is undoubtedly much more beneficial for men to live by the laws and sure dictates of their reason, which aim at man's true benefit. Now everyone tries to live as much as he can without fear. This, however, is impossible as long as everyone is free to do as he likes, with as much right to hatred and anger as to reason; 13. for everybody lives anxiously who lives amid enmity, hate, anger and deceit, and does his best to avoid them. Seeing, then, that in the absence of mutual help the lives of men are bound (as I explained in Ch. V) to be wretched and to leave no scope for the cultivation of reason, it is obvious that in order to live safely and at their best they had to unite and take steps to ensure that the right which by nature they possessed singly should be possessed collectively, and so be determined no longer by the force and appetite of each individual but by the power and will of all of them together. 14. Such a project would have been quite futile if they had gone on following only their appetites, since these draw men in different directions. Therefore they had to make an indefeasible compact to regulate all their affairs only at the bidding of reason (which nobody dares to repudiate openly, lest he seem to be wanting in mental capacity), to bridle their appetites so far as these lead to the hurt of other persons, to refrain from doing to others what they would not

neminique facere quod sibi fieri non vult, iusque denique alterius tamquam suum defendere.

15. Qua autem ratione pactum hoc iniri debeat ut ratum fixumque sit hic iam videndum. Nam lex humanae naturae universalis est ut nemo aliquod quod bonum esse iudicat neglegat nisi spe maioris boni vel ex metu maioris damni, nec aliquid malum perferat nisi ad maius evitandum vel spe maioris boni; hoc est, unusquisque de duobus bonis quod ipse maius esse iudicat, & de duobus malis quod minus sibi videtur eliget. Dico expresse quod sibi eligenti maius aut minus videtur, non quod res necessario ita se habeat ut ipse iudicat. 16. Atque haec lex adeo firmiter naturae humanae inscripta est ut inter aeternas veritates sit ponenda quas nemo ignorare potest. At ex ea necessario sequitur neminem absque dolo promissurum se iure quod in omnia habet cessurum, & absolute neminem promissis staturum, nisi ex metu maioris mali vel spe maioris boni.... 20. Ex quibus concludimus pactum nullam vim habere posse nisi ratione utilitatis, qua sublata pactum simul tollitur & irritum manet. Ac propterea stulte alterius fidem in aeternum sibi aliquem expostulare si simul non conatur efficere ut ex ruptione pacti ineundi plus damni quam utilitatis ruptorem sequatur; quod quidem in republica instituenda maxime locum habere debet.

21. At si omnes homines facile solo ductu rationis duci possent summamque reipublicae utilitatem & necessitatem noscere, nullus esset qui dolos prorsus non detestaretur; sed omnes summa cum fide ex cupiditate summi huius boni, nempe reipublicae conservandae, pactis omnino starent, & fidem, summum reipublicae praesidium, supra omnia servarent. 22. Sed longe abest ut omnes ex solo ductu rationis facile semper duci possint, nam unusquisque a sua voluptate trahitur,* & avaritia gloria invidia ira &c. saepissime mens ita occupatur ut nullus locus rationi reliquatur. 23. Quapropter quamvis homines

---

* Cf. Virg., *Ecl.* II, 65.

wish others to do to themselves, and to defend other men's rights as if these were their own.

15. We must now see in what way such a compact has to be entered into if it is to be made lastingly valid and effective. It is a general law of human nature that no one will do without anything he deems to be good except in the hope of a greater good or through fear of a greater loss, and that no one will endure an evil except to avoid a greater one or in the hope of a compensating good, i.e. everybody chooses what seems to him to be the greater of two goods or the lesser of two evils. Note that I say explicitly, greater or lesser in his own eyes, not necessarily in reality. **16.** That law is so deeply engraved in human nature that it must be included in those eternal truths of which nobody can be ignorant. Hence nobody, except in deceit, will promise to surrender his right to everything, and nobody without exception will keep his promises, except through fear of a greater evil or hope of a greater good... **20.** From these considerations I infer that a compact has no force except so far as it is beneficial, so that if the benefit ceases the compact ceases with it and remains void. It is therefore foolish to claim anybody's lasting loyalty to it unless some means be sought of ensuring that any breach of it will bring more harm than good on him that breaks it. The finding of such a means is of the highest importance in the establishment of a State.

21. If it were easy for everybody to be led by nothing but reason, and to perceive the supreme necessity and benefit of a State, everybody would thoroughly detest deceit, and through desire for that highest good (i.e. the preservation of the State) would loyally stand by the compact and maintain this loyalty, the State's chief protection, before everything else. **22.** That it is easy for everybody to follow nothing but reason is, however, nowhere near the truth; everyone is captivated by what he regards as pleasant, and greed, ambition, envy, anger etc. so often hold his mind that no room is left for reason. **23.** Accordingly, although men may with an appearance

certis signis simplicis animi promittant & paciscantur se fidem servaturos, nemo tamen nisi promisso aliud accedat de fide alterius potest esse certus.... 24. Verum quia iam ostendimus ius naturale sola potentia uniuscuiusque determinari, sequitur quod quantum unusquisque potentiae quam habet in alterum vel vi vel sponte transfert tantum etiam de suo iure alteri necessario cedere, & illum summum ius in omnes habere qui summam habet potestatem qua omnes vi cogere & metu summi supplicii, quod omnes universaliter timent, retinere potest; quod quidem ius tamdiu tantum retinebit quamdiu hanc potentiam quicquid velit exsequendi conservabit, alias precario imperabit & nemo fortior, nisi velit, ei obtemperare tenebitur.

25. Hac itaque ratione sine ulla naturalis iuris repugnantia societas formari potest pactumque omne summa cum fide semper servari, si nimirum unusquisque omnem quam habet potentiam in societatem transferat, quae adeo summum naturae ius in omnia, hoc est summum imperium sola retinebit, cui unusquisque vel ex libero animo vel metu summi supplicii parere tenebitur. 26. Talis vero societatis ius democratia vocatur, quae proinde definitur coetus universus hominum qui collegialiter summum ius ad omnia quae potest habet. Ex quo sequitur summam potestatem nulla lege teneri, sed omnes ad omnia ei parere debere, hoc enim tacite vel expresse pacisci debuerunt omnes, cum omnem suam potentiam se defendendi, hoc est omne suum ius, in eam transtulerunt. 27. Quippe si aliquid sibi servatum volebant, debuerant simul sibi cavere quo id tuto defendere possent; cum autem id non fecerint nec absque imperii divisione & consequenter destructione facere potuerint, eo ipso se arbitrio summae potestatis absolute summiserunt; quod cum absolute fecerint idque (ut iam ostendi-

of sincerity promise, and formally contract, to keep good faith, nobody can be certain of the loyalty of anybody else unless there is something besides the mere promise.... 24. Now each man's natural right being, I have explained, limited only by his power, so far as he transfers this to someone else (whether under compulsion or freely) he necessarily transfers with it so much of his right; and that man has supreme right over other men who has the supreme power by which he is able forcibly to coerce them, or to restrain them by the fear of capital punishment which is common to all men; and he retains that right only so long as he in fact continues to have the power to carry out whatever measures he pleases, for otherwise his rule would be precarious, no stronger man being obliged against his own will to obey him.

25. The way in which a society can be formed, and the compact be wholly and lastingly kept, with complete loyalty and yet with no violation of natural right, is, then, that every individual shall transfer all his power to the society as a whole, which will then alone hold the supreme right to everything, i.e. the sovereign authority which every individual will be obliged to obey, whether freely or through fear of capital punishment. 26. A society with such a right is called a democracy, which may be defined as a general union of men that possesses collectively the supreme right to everything which it has the effectual power to do. Evidently, the Supreme Power will not be bound by any law; conversely, all the members of the society are under obligation to be completely obedient to it, for in the compact they had all to pledge themselves, tacitly or explicitly, to be so when they transferred to it all their power of self-defence and therefore all their right. 27. If they had wished to reserve to themselves any part of their right, they should have taken care to provide for its protection. As they did not do so, and could not without dividing and so destroying the State, they were submitting unconditionally to the will of the Supreme Power; and as they did take this step, and took it (as we have shown) under the pressure of

mus) & necessitate cogente & ipsa ratione suadente, hinc sequitur quod nisi hostes imperii esse velimus & contra rationem imperium summis viribus defendere suadentem agere, omnia absolute summae potestatis mandata exsequi tenemur, tametsi absurdissima imperet, talia enim ratio exsequi etiam iubet ut de duobus malis minus eligamus.

28. Adde quod hoc periculum se scilicet alterius imperio & arbitrio absolute summittendi facile unusquisque adire poterat, nam, ut ostendimus, summis potestatibus hoc ius quicquid velint imperandi tamdiu tantum competit quamdiu revera summam habet potestatem, quod si eandem amiserint simul etiam ius omnia imperandi amittunt, & in eum vel eos cadit qui ipsum acquisiverunt & retinere possunt. 29. Quapropter raro admodum contingere potest ut summae potestates absurdissima imperent, ipsis enim maxime incumbit ut sibi prospiciant & imperium retineant communi bono consulere & omnia ex rationis dictamina dirigere; violenta enim imperia, ut ait Seneca, nemo continuit diu. 30. Quibus accedit quod in democratico imperio minus timenda sunt absurda. Nam fere impossibile est ut maior unius coetus pars si magnus est in uno absurdo conveniat; deinde propter eius fundamentum & finem qui, ut etiam ostendimus, nullus alius est quam absurda appetitus vitare & homines sub rationis limites quoad eius fieri potest continere, ut concorditer & pacifice vivant; quod fundamentum si tollatur facile tota fabrica ruet. 31. His ergo providere summae tantum potestati incumbit, subditis autem, uti diximus, eius mandata exsequi nec aliud ius agnoscere quam quod summa potestas ius esse declarat.

32. At forsan aliquis putabit nos hac ratione subditos servos facere, quia putant servum esse eum qui ex mandato agit, & liberum qui animo suo morem gerit; quod quidem non absolute verum est, nam revera is qui a sua voluptate ita trahitur & nihil quod sibi utile est videre neque agere potest maxime servus est, & solus ille liber qui integro animo ex solo ductu ra-

necessity and the guidance of reason, we too—unless we wish to be hostile to the State, acting against reason, which bids us defend the State with all our might—are unconditionally obliged to carry out all the commands of the Supreme Power, even if they be utterly foolish; for reason bids us do so as the lesser of two evils.

28. The risk involved in unconditional submission to the dominion and will of another was something that could be faced without misgiving, for, as we have seen, the power of ruling as it pleases belongs to a Supreme Power only so long as it has in fact the supreme power, so that when it loses this it loses at the same time the right to command everything, which then passes to him or those who have acquired it and are able to keep it. 29. For this reason a Supreme Power will scarcely ever command anything utterly foolish; in order to watch its own interest and retain its dominion, its chief business is to attend to the public welfare and rule in a rational way. As Seneca says, "No despotic government lasts long." 30. Under a democratic government there is less risk of foolish ordinances, since it is nearly impossible for a majority in a large assembly to concur in a foolish decision. After all, the very ground or purpose of a State is to avert the follies of appetite and confine men as far as possible within the bounds of reason, so that they may live together in peace and concord. If this purpose is lost, the whole structure quickly falls to pieces. 31. To provide for these matters is the duty of the Supreme Power and of it alone, the duty of the subjects being to follow its commands and recognise nothing as law but what it proclaims to be such.

32. It may be objected that I am turning subjects into slaves. The objection supposes that a slave is a person who acts under orders, and a free man one who acts of his own accord. This is not altogether true, for anybody who is dragged along by lust for pleasure, unable to see or do what is good for him, is more a slave than anybody else; and the only man who is really free is one who lives entirely and willingly by

tionis vivit. 33. Actio autem ex mandato, hoc est oboedientia, libertatem quidem aliquo modo tollit, at non ilico servum facit sed actionis ratio. Si finis actionis non est ipsius agentis sed imperantis utilitas, tum agens servus est & sibi inutilis. 34. At in republica & imperio ubi salus totius populi non imperantis summa lex est, qui in omnibus summae potestati obtemperat non sibi inutilis servus sed subditus dicendus; & ideo illa respublica maxime libera est cuius leges sana ratione fundatae sunt, ibi enim unusquisque ubi velit liber esse potest, hoc est integro animo ex ductu rationis vivere.

36. Atque his imperii democratici fundamenta satis clare ostendisse puto, de quo prae omnibus agere malui quia maxime naturale videbatur & maxime ad libertatem quam natura unicuique concedit accedere; nam in eo nemo ius suum naturale ita in alterum transfert ut nulla sibi in posterum consultatio sit, sed in maiorem totius societatis partem cuius ille unam facit; atque hac ratione omnes manent ut antea in statu naturali aequales.

37. Deinde de hoc solo imperio ex professo agere volui quia ad meum intentum maxime facit qui de utilitate libertatis in republica agere constitueram. Reliquarum ergo potestatum fundamentis supersedeo nec nobis ut earum ius noscamus scire iam opus est unde ortum habuerint & saepe habeant, id enim ex modo ostensis satis superque constat. 38. Nam quisquis summam habet potestatem, sive unus sit sive pauci sive denique omnes, certum est ei summum ius quicquid velit imperandi competere; & praeterea quisquis potestatem se defendendi sive sponte sive vi coactus in alium transtulit eum suo iure naturali plane cessisse & consequenter eidem ad omnia absolute parere decrevisse, quod omnino praestare tenetur

reason. 33. Acting under orders—i.e. obedience—does of course take away some liberty. It is not, however, this aspect of an action but the aim of it that makes a man a slave. If the aim is the good not of him that is acting but of him that is commanding, the former is a slave, of no use to himself. 34. But in a State where the supreme principle of law is the welfare not of the ruler but of the whole body of the people, he who completely obeys the Supreme Power is to be called not a slave, never doing anything for his own benefit, but a subject. That State is therefore the freest in which the laws are based on sound reason, for there every citizen can be free if he so wills, i.e. can himself live sincerely under the guidance of reason.

36. I have, I think, sufficiently indicated the basis of a democratic State, which I have preferred to consider because it seems to be the most natural one, approaching most nearly the freedom which nature gives to us all; for in it nobody transfers his natural right to another in such a way as to be unable thereafter ever to consult his own interest, but transfers it to the majority in a society of which he is himself a part. By this method of government, then, all remain equal, as they were in their natural condition.

37. Another reason why I have explicitly discussed this form of government alone is that it is the one that best serves my purpose, which is, as I stated earlier, to consider the benefit of freedom in a State. I pass over the other forms of government, there being no need to inquire separately into their origin in order to ascertain what right they had and often still have, since this should be abundantly evident from what has just been said. 38. Whoever has the supreme power, whether one man, a few, or all, has the supreme right to command whatever he wills; and whoever has transferred to another, whether freely or under compulsion, his power of defending himself, has thereby surrendered also his natural right, and in so doing has by implication resolved to give to the other unconditional obedience in all matters, an obedience that re-

quamdiu rex sive nobiles sive populus summam quam acceperunt potestatem quae iuris transferendi fundamentum fuit conservant....

39. Imperii fundamentis & iure ostensis, facile erit determinare quid ius civile privatum, quid iniuria quid iustitia & iniustitia in statu civili sit.... **40.** Per ius enim civile privatum nihil aliud intellegere possumus quam uniuscuiusque libertatem ad sese in suo statu conservandum, quae edictis summae potestatis determinatur solaque eiusdem auctoritate defenditur. Nam postquam unusquisque ius suum ex proprio beneplacito vivendi quo sola sua potestate determinabatur, hoc est suam libertatem & potentiam se defendendi, in alium transtulit, ex sola illius ratione iam vivere tenetur & solo eiusdem praesidio se defendere. **41.** Iniuria est cum civis vel subditus ab alio aliquod damnum contra ius civile sive edictum summae potestatis pati cogitur. Iniuria enim non nisi in statu civili potest concipi. Sed neque a summis potestatibus quibus iure omnia licent ulla fieri potest subditis; ergo in privatis tantum qui iure tenentur invicem non laedere locum habere potest. **42.** Iustitia est animi constantia tribuendi unicuique quod ei ex iure civili competit. Iniustitia autem est specie iuris alicui detrahere quod ei ex vera legum interpretatione competit. Vocantur etiam aequitas & iniquitas quia qui constituti sunt ad lites dirimendas nullum respectum personarum sed omnes aequales habere tenentur & ius uniuscuiusque aeque defendere, non diviti invidere neque pauperem contemnere.

61. Si quis autem roget, quid si summa potestas aliquid contra religionem & oboedientiam quam Deo expresso pacto promisimus imperet, divino an humano imperio obtemperandum? Sed quia de his in sequentibus prolixius agam, hic bre-

mains obligatory as long as the monarch, the nobles, or the people retain effectively the supreme power which had been given to them and which was the basis of the transference of right....

39. The grounds and right of government having been expounded, we can now define easily what private civil right is, and what wrong, justice, and injustice are in the political order.... 40. Private civil right can only mean each individual's freedom to preserve his life and nature so far as this freedom is defined by the edicts, and protected solely by the authority, of the Supreme Power; for when each individual has transferred to another his right, hitherto limited only by his power, to live as he pleases, i.e. his freedom and power of self-defence, he is obliged to live only by the reason, and defend himself only with the arm, of that person. 41. There is civil wrong when a citizen or subject has to suffer at the hands of another person some hurt that is contrary to civil right, i.e. to an edict of the Supreme Power. It is therefore possible only in a State. It cannot, however, be committed on the subjects by the Supreme Power, this having the right to do anything, but only by private persons on one another, these being obliged in law to do no hurt to one another. 42. Justice is the settled disposition to give everyone that to which his civil right entitles him. Injustice is to deprive anyone, under the pretext of a right, of that to which he is entitled on a true interpretation of the laws. Justice and injustice are also called equity and inequity, because those who are appointed to adjudicate in lawsuits are required to have no respect of persons, but to regard all the parties as equal and defend the right of each equally, neither begrudging anything to the rich nor despising the poor.

61. Suppose anyone should at this point ask, "What if the Supreme Power commands something contrary to religion and to the obedience which we have expressly promised to God in the compact? Ought we to obey the divine or the human command?" Since I shall be dealing with this question

viter tantum dico Deo supra omnia oboediendum quando certam & indubitatam habemus revelationem. 62. Sed quia circa religionem maxime errare solent homines & pro ingeniorum diversitate multa magno certamine fingere, ut experientia plus quam satis testatur, certum est quod si nemo summae potestati iure teneretur obtemperare in iis quae ipse ad religionem pertinere putat, tum ius civitatis a diverso uniuscuiusque iudicio & adfectu penderet. 63. Nam nemo eodem teneretur qui id contra suam fidem & superstitionem statutum iudicaret, atque adeo unusquisque sub hoc praetextu licentiam ad omnia sumere posset; & quando quidem hac ratione ius civitatis prorsus violatur, hinc sequitur summae potestati, cui soli iura imperii conservare & tutari tam iure divino quam naturali incumbit, ius summum competere de religione statuendi quicquid iudicat & omnes ad eiusdem de eadem decreta & mandata ex fide ipsi data quam Deus omnino servari iubet obtemperare teneri.

CAP. XVII

1. Contemplatio praecedentis Capitis de iure summarum potestatum in omnia, deque iure naturali uniuscuiusque in easdem translato, quamvis cum praxi non parum conveniat & praxis ita institui possit ut ad eandem magis ac magis accedat, numquam tamen fiet quin in multis mere theoretica maneat. 2. Nam nemo umquam suam potentiam & consequenter neque suum ius ita in alium transferre poterit ut homo esse desinat, nec talis ulla summa potestas umquam dabitur quae omnia ita ut vult exsequi possit. Frustra enim subdito imperaret ut illum odio habeat qui eum sibi beneficio iunxit, ut amet qui ei

later at some length, I need only say here that obedience to God is higher than any other when we are in possession of a definite and undoubted revelation. 62. It is, however, in matters of religion that men most often err, and because of their different mentalities frame many different views and dispute much about them, as experience amply testifies. If, then, nobody were obliged by right to obey the Supreme Power in any matter which he himself regards as bearing on religion, the right of the State would depend on everybody's various judgments and feelings; 63. for no one would be obliged by that right if he deemed its statutory expression to be contrary to his faith and devotion, and on this pretext everyone could claim the liberty to do anything. Now since thereby the right of the State would be grossly violated, we must grant that the Supreme Power, being alone charged, by divine as well as natural right, with preserving the rights of government, is entitled to make such decrees as it pleases about religious matters; and that everybody is obliged by his pledge to the Supreme Power, which God orders to be rigidly kept, to obey in those matters the commands of that Power.

CH. XVII. THE PRACTICAL LIMITATIONS OF SOVEREIGNTY

1. Although what has been said in the preceding chapter about the right of the Supreme Power to everything, and about the natural right transferred to that Power by every individual, agrees fairly well with actual practice, and although practice could be made to approximate ever more closely to it, it always remains in many respects a merely theoretical truth. 2. Nobody can in fact so transfer to someone else his power, and therefore his right, as to cease to be a human being, nor will there ever be a Supreme Power able to carry out all its wishes. No command of any Supreme Power could make a man hate someone to whom he is attached by an act of kindness, or like someone who has done him a wrong, or

damnum intulit, ut contumeliis non offendatur, ut a metu liberari non cupiat, & alia perplurima huiusmodi quae ex legibus humanae naturae necessario sequuntur. 3. Atque hoc ipsam etiam experientiam clarissime docere existimo. Nam numquam homines suo iure ita cesserunt, suamque potentiam in alium ita transtulerunt, ut ab iis ipsis qui eorum ius & potentiam acceperunt non timerentur, & imperium non magis propter cives quamquam suo iure privatos quam propter hostes periclitaretur. 4. Et sane si homines iure suo naturali ita privari possent ut nihil in posterum possent nisi volentibus iis qui supremum ius retinuerunt, tum profecto impune violentissime in subditos regnare liceret, quod nemini in mentem venire posse credo....

5. Attamen ut recte intellegatur quousque imperii ius & potestas se extendat, notandum imperii potestatem non in eo praecise contineri quod homines metu cogere potest, sed absolute in omnibus quibus efficere potest ut homines eius mandatis obsequantur; non enim ratio obtemperandi sed obtemperantia subditum facit. 6. Nam quacumque ratione homo deliberet summae potestatis mandata exsequi, sive ideo sit quod poenam timet sive quod aliquid inde sperat sive quod patriam amat sive alio quocumque adfectu impulsus, tamen ex proprio suo consilio deliberat, & nihilo minus ex summae potestatis imperio agit. 7. Non igitur ex eo quod homo proprio consilio aliquid facit ilico concludendum eum id ex suo & non imperii iure agere. Nam quando quidem tam cum ex amore obligatus quam cum metu coactus ad malum evitandum, semper ex proprio consilio & decreto agit, vel imperium nullum esset nec ullum ius in subditos, vel id necessario ad omnia se extendit quibus effici potest ut homines ipsi cedere deliberent, & consequenter quicquid subditus facit quod mandatis summae potestatis respondet, sive id amore obligatus sive metu coercitus

not be offended by insults, or not desire to be free from fear, and many other such things, which are all necessitated by the laws of human nature. 3. Experience itself, I think, bears this out very clearly. Men have never surrendered their right and power to such an extent as not to be feared by those who have received them. States have always been more in danger from their citizens, although these have lost their right, than from their enemies. 4. If men could in fact be deprived of their natural right so completely as thereafter to be able to do nothing at all except by the will of those who hold the Sovereign Right, then these could indeed rule with utter tyranny over their subjects with impunity; but this is a possibility which, I am sure, no one could entertain....

5. If we are to conceive correctly how far the right and power of government extend, we must see that its power is not confined to coercing men through fear, but covers everything it can in fact do to make them obedient to its commands; for is the *fact* of obedience, not the manner or cause, that makes one a subject. 6. Whatever it be that leads a man to decide to carry out the command of the Supreme Power—whether fear of punishment, hope of benefit, love of country, or any other motive—he decides on the basis of his own reflection; yet, after all, his ensuing action is done because of the authority of the Supreme Power. 7. It would be wrong to infer that because a man does what he does after personal reflection he is doing it by his own right, not by the right of the ruler. We do in fact always act on the basis of our own reflection and by our own decision, whether we are bound by affection or restrained by fear, from which it follows either that there is no such thing as rule or right over subjects, or else that it necessarily extends to all the means by which men can be brought by their own decision to yield to it. What follows from this second alternative is that whatever a subject does in external accordance with the commands of the Supreme Power he does by the latter's right, not by his own, whether he is acting through affection or under the coercion of fear,

sive (quod quidem magis frequens) ex spe & metu simul, sive ex reverentia quae passio est ex metu & admiratione composita, sive quacumque ratione ductus, ex iure imperii non autem suo agit. 8. Quod etiam hinc quam clarissime constat quod oboedientia non tam externam quam animi internam actionem respiciat; adeoque ille maxime sub alterius imperio est qui alteri integro animo ad omnia eius mandata obtemperare deliberat, & consequenter eum maximum tenere imperium qui in subditorum animos regnat. Quod si qui maxime timentur maximum tenerent imperium, tum profecto id tyrannorum subditi tenerent qui a suis tyrannis maxime timentur. 9. Deinde quamvis non perinde animis ac linguis imperari possit, sunt tamen animi aliqua ratione sub imperio summae potestatis, quae multis modis efficere potest ut permagna hominum pars quicquid vult credat amet odio habeat &c. 10. Adeoque etsi haec non directo mandato summae potestatis fiant, fiunt tamen saepe, ut experientia abunde testatur, ex auctoritate ipsius potentiae & ipsius directione, id est ex ipsius iure...

13. Quod imperii conservatio praecipue pendeat a subditorum fide eorumque virtute & animi constantia in exsequendis mandatis, ratio & experientia quam clarissime docent; qua autem ratione iidem duci debeant ut fidem & virtutem constanter servent non aeque facile est videre. 14. Omnes namque tam qui regunt quam qui reguntur homines sunt ex labore scilicet proclives ad libidinem. Immo qui tantum varium multitudinis ingenium experti sunt de eo fere desperant; quia non ratione sed solis adfectibus gubernatur, praeceps ad omnia & facillime vel avaritia vel luxu corrumpitur. 15. Unusquisque solus omnia se scire putat & omnia ex suo ingenio moderari vult, & eatenus aequum vel iniquum fasque nefasque existimat quatenus in suum lucrum vel damnum cadere iudicat, prae gloria aequales contemnit, nec ab iis dirigi patitur, prae invidia melioris laudis vel fortunae quae numquam aequalis est malum alterius cupit

or (as usually happens) through both at the same time, or through respect, which is a mixture of fear and admiration, or through any other motive. 8. This is quite evident from the fact that obedience means not so much an external as an internal act of the mind. Consequently, that man is most under the rule of another who decides to obey willingly all the latter's commands; and conversely he is most unequivocally a ruler who rules his subjects' minds—though if the strongest rulers were the men who are most feared, rule would really belong to the *subjects* of tyrants, since tyrants fear them greatly. 9. Although minds cannot be ruled as tongues can be, they are to some extent under the dominion of the Supreme Power, for this is able in a variety of ways to determine what the great majority of its subjects shall wish, believe, like, hate and so on. 10. While this does not occur by the direct command of the Sovereign Power, experience amply proves that it occurs often because of the influence of the Sovereign's power and control, and therefore because of the Sovereign's right....

13. That the preservation of a State depends chiefly on the loyalty of the subjects in obeying the laws conscientiously and consistently, is the plain testimony of both reason and experience. By what methods the subjects can be led to this obedience is not, however, so evident. 14. For both rulers and ruled are human, prone to run away from the hard to the pleasant. The fickleness of mind of the masses drives anyone who has much to do with it nearly to despair, for they are governed not by reason but only by their passions; ready to rush into anything, they are easily seduced by greed and sensuality. 15. Besides, every individual supposes that he alone knows everything, and wants to arrange everything to his own satisfaction; counts anything just or unjust, legitimate or illegitimate, according as he thinks it relevant to his gain or loss; out of pride despises his equals, refusing to accept directions from them; and out of envy of the greater reputation or good fortune (which is never equal) of other men he wishes them misfortune, and if this befalls takes delight in it. There is no

eoque delectatur; nec opus est omnia recensere. 16. Norunt quippe omnes quid sceleris fastidium praesentium & rerum novandarum cupiditas, quid praeceps ira, quid contempta paupertas frequenter suadeant hominibus, quantumque eorum animos occupent agitentque. His ergo omnibus praevenire & imperium ita constituere ut nullus locus fraudi relinquatur, immo omnia ita instituere ut omnes cuiuscumque ingenii sint ius publicum privatis commodis praeferant, hoc opus hic labor est. 17. Rei quidem necessitas multa excogitare coegit, attamen numquam eo perventum est ut imperium non magis propter cives quam hostes periclitaretur, & qui id tenent non magis illos quam hos timerent. 18. Testis invictissima ab hostibus Romanorum respublica toties a suis civibus victa & miserrima oppressa....

CAP. XIX

1. Cum supra dixi eos qui imperium tenent ius ad omnia solos habere & a solo eorum decreto ius omne pendere, non tantum civile intellegere volui sed etiam sacrum; nam huius etiam & interpretes esse debent & vindices. Atque hoc hic expresse notare volo & de eo ex professo in hoc Capite agere, quia plurima sunt qui pernegant hoc ius, nempe circa sacra, summis potestatibus competere neque eas interpretes iuris divini agnoscere volunt; 2. unde etiam licentiam sibi sumunt easdem accusandi & traducendi ...Sed eos hac ratione imperium dividere, immo viam ad imperium adfectare infra in hoc ipso Capite videbimus; nam prius ostendere volo religionem vim iuris accipere ex solo eorum decreto qui ius imperandi habent, & Deum nullum singulare regnum in homines habere nisi per eos qui imperium tenent, & praeterea quod religionis cultus & pietatis exercitium reipublicae paci & utilitati accommodari & consequenter a solis summis potestatibus determinari

need to complete the review. 16. Everybody knows well what wicked deeds often result from disgust with the existing state of affairs, desire for a change, rash anger, and the humiliation of poverty, and how much these grip and disturb the mind. To guard against all these and establish a State that, besides leaving no room for evasion of the law, leads all the citizens, whatever their dispositions, to put public right before private convenience—this is the great need, this the great task. 17. Necessity has indeed been the mother of invention; yet never has there been a State that was not in greater peril from its citizens than from its external enemies, and whose rulers did not fear those more than these. 18. Rome is an example—undefeated by her enemies, yet often defeated and reduced to misery by her own citizens.

CH. XIX. THE RIGHT OF RULERS OVER MORALITY AND RELIGION

1. When I said that rulers, and they alone, have a right to everything, all right depending exclusively on their decree, I meant religious as well as civil right: of the former too they should be both the interpreters and the guardians. I take up this point for special treatment in this Chapter because there are many who strongly deny that right over religious matters belongs to the Supreme Power, and who, not recognising the latter as the interpreter of religious law, 2. arrogate to themselves the liberty to arraign rulers publicly.... That they are thereby dividing the State, indeed paving the way for their own usurpation of it, we shall see later in this chapter. What I first wish to prove is that religion acquires the force of law solely by the decree of those who have the right of rule, and that God has no peculiar rule over men except through temporal rulers; and further, that religious rites and duties should be in accordance with the peace and welfare of the State, and therefore be determined, and consequently inter-

debet, quaeque adeo eius etiam interpretes debent esse. 3. Loquor expresse de pietatis exercitio & externo religionis cultu, non autem de ipsa pietate & Dei interno cultu sive mediis quibus mens interne disponitur ad Deum integritate animi colendum; internus enim Dei cultus & ipsa pietas uniuscuiusque iuris est quod in alium transferri non potest. 4. Porro quid hic per Dei regnum intellegam ex Cap. XIV satis constare existimo, in eo enim ostendimus eum legem Dei adimplere qui iustitiam & caritatem ex Dei mandato colit; unde sequitur illud regnum esse Dei in quo iustitia & caritas vim iuris & mandati habent. 5. Atque hic nullam agnosco differentiam sive Deus verum iustitiae & caritatis cultum lumine naturali sive revelatione doceat imperetque; nihil enim refert quomodo ille cultus revelatus sit modo summum ius obtineat summaque lex hominibus sit.

6. Si igitur iam ostendam iustitiam & caritatem vim iuris & mandati non posse accipere nisi ex iure imperii, facile inde concludam (quando quidem ius imperii penes summas potestates tantum est) religionem vim iuris accipere ex solo eorum decreto qui ius imperandi habent, & Deum nullum singulare regnum in homines habere nisi per eos qui imperium tenent. 7. At quod cultus iustitiae & caritatis vim iuris non accipit nisi ex iure imperii ex antecedentibus patet; ostendimus enim Cap. XVI in statu naturali non plus iuris rationi quam appetitui esse, sed tam eos qui secundum leges appetitus quam eos qui secundum leges rationis vivunt ius ad omnia quae possunt habere. 8. Hac de causa in statu naturali peccatum concipere non potuimus, nec Deum tamquam iudicem homines propter peccata punientem, sed omnia secundum leges universae naturae communes ferri <?fieri>, & eundem casum (ut cum Salomone loquar) iusto ac impio, puro ac impuro &c. contingere, & nul-

preted, by the Supreme Power. 3. Observe that I am writing only of the external forms of worship and religious duty, not of piety itself and the inner worship of God, or of the means by which the mind is inwardly brought to worship God in sincerity, for religion in this intimate form is a part of the right of every individual that cannot be alienated. 4. What I mean by the kingdom of God has, I think, been made clear in Ch. XIV, in which I argued that the fulfilment of God's law consists in the cultivation of justice and charity on the ground that God requires them. A kingdom is God's, then, in which justice and charity have the force of law. 5. Whether the true way of practising justice and charity be divinely made known and commanded by the natural light of reason or by revelation is in our present context irrelevant; what matters is not how it is made known but that it should have the supreme authority and be in fact the supreme law.

6. If, then, I now demonstrate that justice and charity cannot acquire the force of law and ordinance except from the right of government, it will be a short step to infer (since the right of government lies only with the Supreme Power) that religion acquires the force of law solely from the decree of those who hold the right to govern, and that God has no peculiar rule over men except through temporal rulers. 7. Now it is evident from my earlier discussion that the practice of justice and charity does not acquire the force of law except from the right of government; for I proved in Ch. XVI that in man's natural condition reason has no more right than appetite has, so that those who live in accordance with the laws of appetite, just as much as those who live in accordance with the laws of reason, have the right to do everything they are able to do. 8. Consequently, in man's natural condition the idea of sin, and with it the idea of God as a judge punishing men for their sins, have no application: we have to think of everything as happening in accordance with universal laws of nature as a whole, say with Solomon that the same lot happens to the righteous and the wicked, to the pure and the impure, and

lum locum iustitiae & caritati esse. At ut verae rationis documenta, hoc est (ut in Cap. IV circa legem divinam ostendimus) ipsa divina documenta, vim iuris absolute haberent, necesse fuisse ut unusquisque iure suo naturali cederet & omnes idem in omnes vel in aliquot vel in unum transferrent; & tum demum nobis primum innotuit quid iustitia quid iniustitia quid aequitas quidque iniquitas esset. 9. Iustitia igitur & absolute omnia verae rationis documenta & consequenter erga proximum caritas a solo imperii iure, hoc est a solo eorum decreto qui ius imperandi habent, vim iuris & mandati accipiunt; & quia in solo iustitiae & caritatis sive verae religionis iure Dei regnum consistit, sequitur, ut volebamus, Deum nullum regnum in homines habere nisi per eos qui imperium tenent....

18. ... Ibi <Cap. IV> enim ostendimus Dei decreta aeternam veritatem & necessitatem omnia involvere, nec posse concipi Deum tamquam principem vel legislatorem leges hominibus ferentem. 19. Quapropter divina documenta lumine naturali vel prophetico revelata vim mandati a Deo immediate non accipiunt, sed necessario ab iis vel mediantibus iis qui ius imperandi & decretandi habent; adeoque non nisi mediantibus iisdem concipere possumus Deum in homines regnare resque humanas secundum iustitiam & aequitatem dirigere, quod ipsa etiam experientia comprobatur. 20. Nam nulla divinae iustitiae vestigia reperiuntur nisi ubi iusti regnant, alias (ut Salomonis verba iterum repetam) eundem casum iusto ac iniusto puro ac impuro contingere videmus; quod quidem plurimos qui Deum in homines immediate regnare & totam naturam in eorum usum dirigere putabant de divina providentia dubitare fecit. 21. Cum itaque tam experientia quam ratione constet ius divinum a solo decreto summarum potestatum pendere, sequitur easdem etiam eiusdem esse interpretes, qua autem ratione iam videbimus.

Nam tempus est ut ostendamus cultum religionis externum & omne pietatis exercitium reipublicae paci & conservationi

hold that justice and charity have no place. The precepts of true reason, which (as I showed in Ch. IV when discussing divine law) are the very precepts of God, could have the full force of law only because every individual surrendered his natural right, transferring it to all collectively, or to a few, or to one man. Only then did we come to know what justice and injustice are, and what equity and inequity. 9. Therefore all the precepts of true reason—justice, charity to one's neighbour, and the rest—acquire the force of law and ordinance solely from the decree of those who have the right of rule; and since the kingdom of God is purely the rightful sway of justice and charity, i.e. of true religion, God has no rule over men except through those who hold earthly Sovereignty....

18.... I argued in Ch. IV that all the decrees of God involve eternal truth and necessity, and that God cannot be conceived after the analogy of one who rules over men or legislates for them. 19. Therefore the divine precepts, whether made known to us by reason or by prophecy, do not acquire the force of ordinances directly from God but, of necessity, from or through those who have the right to rule and make decrees. It is only through the mediation of such men, then, that we can think of God as ruling over us and directing human affairs in accordance with justice and equity. Experience confirms this conclusion. 20. We find in fact that divine justice shows itself only where there are just rulers. Where there are not, we see (if I may quote Solomon again) the righteous and the unrighteous, the pure and the impure, suffering the same lot, a fact that led many of those who supposed that God rules over men directly and orders the whole of nature for their benefit to excite doubts about divine providence. 21. Since, then, it is evident by experience as well as by reason that divine law depends solely on the decree of the Supreme Power, this must be the interpreter of it—in what respect we shall see presently.

We must now prove that, if we wish to obey God rightly, religion and morality in their external forms should be adjusted

debere accommodari, si recte Deo obtemperare velimus. Hoc autem demonstrato facile intellegemus qua ratione summae potestates interpretes religionis & pietatis sunt. 22. Certum est quod pietas erga patriam summa sit quam aliquis praestare potest, nam sublato imperio nihil boni potest consistere sed omnia in discrimen veniunt & sola ira & impietas maximo omnium metu regnat; unde sequitur nihil proximo pium praestari posse quod non impium sit si inde damnum totius reipublicae sequatur, & contra nihil in eundem impium committi quod pietati non tribuatur si propter reipublicae conservationem fiat. 24. Cum hoc ita sit, sequitur salutem populi summam esse legem, cui omnes tam humanae quam divinae accommodari debent. At cum solius summae potestatis officium sit determinare quid saluti totius populi & imperii securitati necesse sit et quid necesse esse iudicaverit imperare, hinc sequitur solius etiam summae potestatis officium esse determinare qua ratione unusquisque debet proximum pietate colere, hoc est qua ratione unusquisque Deo oboedire tenetur. 25. Ex his clare intellegimus qua ratione summae potestates interpretes religionis sint....

46. At hic forsan me aliquis rogabit, quisnam ergo si ii qui imperium tenent impii esse velint pietatem iure vindicabit, an tum etiam iidem eius interpretes habendi sunt? Verum ego contra ipsum rogo, quid si ecclesiastici (qui etiam homines sunt & privati, quibus sua tantum negotia curare incumbit) vel alii penes quos ius circa sacra esse vult impii esse velint, an tum etiam eiusdem interpretes habendi sunt? 47. Certum quidem est quod si ii qui imperium tenent qua iuvat ire velint, sive ius circa sacra habeant sive minus, omnia tam sacra quam profana in deterius ruent, & longe citius si qui viri privati seditiose ius divinum vindicare velint.

to the State's need of peace and preservation. The proof of this will enable us to see at once in what respect the Supreme Power is the interpreter of religion and morality. 22. Duty to one's country is certainly the highest moral duty that anyone can perform, for when ordered rule ceases nothing good can stand—everything is in jeopardy, only anger and lawlessness being in charge, with universal fear as the result. Therefore any duty to one's neighbour becomes immoral if it affects adversely the State as a whole; and conversely, whatever is done to him against private duty is public duty if it is done for the preservation of the State. 24. The welfare of the people is thus the highest law, to which all other laws, divine as well as human, should be adjusted. Now since it is the function of the Supreme Power alone to decide what is necessary for the welfare of the people as a whole and for the safety of the State, and to command what he so decides, it is the function of the Supreme Power alone to decide also how each man should do his duty to his neighbour, in other words, how each is to be held to his obedience to God. 25. It should now be clear in what respect the Supreme Power is the interpreter of religion....

46. Someone may now raise the question: "If those who rule choose to be impious, who will then have the right to champion piety? Are they still to be regarded as its interpreters?" To which I reply with a counter-question: "If the ecclesiastics (who also are but human, and private citizens too, whose business is to mind only their own affairs), or any others who may be thought to have control over religious matters, choose to be impious, are they still to be regarded as interpreters of these?" 47. It must be granted that if rulers do choose to proceed as they please, then, whether they have or have not right over religious matters, all affairs, religious and secular alike, will quickly deteriorate; but they will do so much more quickly if private citizens choose to set themselves up seditiously as the guardians of religious law.

CAP. XX

1. Si aeque facile esset animis ac linguis imperare, tuto unusquisque regnaret & nullum imperium violentum foret; nam unusquisque ex imperantium ingenio viveret & ex solo eorum decreto quid verum quid falsum bonum vel malum aequum vel iniquum esset iudicaret. 2. Sed hoc, ut iam in initio Cap. XVII notavimus, fieri nequit, ut scilicet animus alterius iuris absolute sit, quippe nemo ius suum naturale sive facultatem suam libere ratiocinandi & de rebus quibuscumque iudicandi in alium transferre, neque ad id cogi potest. 3. Hinc ergo fit ut illud imperium violentum habeatur quod in animos est, & ut summa maiestas iniuriam subditis facere eorumque ius usurpare videatur quando unicuique praescribere vult quid tamquam verum amplecti & tamquam falsum reicere, & quibus porro opinionibus uniuscuiusque animus erga Deum devotione moveri debeat. Haec enim uniuscuiusque iuris sunt, quo nemo etsi velit cedere potest. 4. Fateor iudicium multis & paene incredibilibus modis praeoccupari posse atque ita ut, quamvis sub alterius imperio directe non sit, tamen ab ore alterius ita pendeat ut merito eatenus eius iuris dici possit. Verum quicquid ars hac in re praestare potuerit numquam tamen eo perventum est ut homines umquam non experirentur unumquemque suo sensu abundare totque capitum quam palatorum esse discrimina.

6. Quantumvis igitur summae potestates ius ad omnia habere & iuris & pietatis interpretes credantur, numquam tamen facere poterunt ne homines iudicium de rebus quibuscumque ex proprio suo ingenio ferant & ne eatenus hoc aut illo adfectu adficiantur. Verum quidem est eas iure posse omnes qui cum iisdem in omnibus absolute non sentiunt pro hostibus habere; sed nos de ipsarum iure iam non disputamus sed de eo quod utile est. 7. Concedo enim easdem iure posse violen-

CH. XX. FREEDOM OF THOUGHT AND SPEECH

1. If it were as easy to control minds as tongues, every ruler would rule quite safely and no State would be oppressive, for all subjects would live as their rulers wish them to do, taking from these all their views about what is true and false, good and bad, just and unjust. 2. But, as was observed at the beginning of Ch. XVII, it is impossible for any mind to be entirely under the control of another, for nobody can transfer to anyone else, whether voluntarily or under compulsion, his natural right to reason freely and form judgments about any matter whatever. 3. This is why any State in which there is rule over minds is regarded as tyrannical, and why a Supreme Power is thought to be doing an injustice to its subjects and to be taking away their right when it sets itself to prescribe what every individual shall accept as true and reject as false, and what religious beliefs he should hold. These matters belong to the right of the individual, which no one is able in fact to surrender, even if he wishes to do so. 4. I admit that a man's judgment can be dominated in many ways, some of them scarcely credible, so that, despite its not being directly at the bidding of another, it may depend so much on the word of another as to warrant our saying that it is to that extent under his jurisdiction. Still, whatever political cunning may have managed to do in that respect, it has never been so successful as to prevent men from being full of their own opinions, or brains from being as different as palates.

6. However much Sovereign Powers may be credited with the right to everything and believed to be the interpreters of law and moral duty, they will never be able to prevent men from coming to their own conclusions about any matter, or from being moved by this or that emotion. It is indeed true that they have the right to regard as enemies all who do not agree with them in every respect. What we are now considering, however, is not their right, but what is politically good. 7. I grant that it is within their right to rule tyrannically, even

tissime regnare & cives levissimis de causis ad necem ducere, at omnes negabunt haec salvo sanae rationis iudicio fieri posse. Immo quia haec non sine magno totius imperii periculo facere queunt, negare etiam possumus easdem absolutam potentiam ad haec & similia habere & consequenter neque etiam absolutum ius; ius enim summarum potestatum ab earum potentia determinari ostendimus.

8. Si itaque nemo libertate sua iudicandi & sentiendi quae vult cedere potest, sed unusquisque maximo naturae iure dominus suarum cogitationum est, sequitur in republica numquam nisi admodum infelici successu temptari posse ut homines quamvis diversa & contraria sentientes nihil tamen nisi ex praescripto summarum potestatum loquantur; nam nec peritissimi ne dicam plebem tacere sciunt. 9. Hoc hominum commune vitium est consilia sua etsi tacito opus est aliis credere. Illud ergo imperium violentissimum erit ubi unicuique libertas dicendi & docendi quae sentit negatur, & contra id moderatum ubi haec eadem libertas unicuique conceditur. 10. Verum enimvero nequaquam etiam negare possumus quin maiestas tam verbis quam re laedi potest, atque adeo, si impossibile est hanc libertatem prorsus adimere subditis, perniciosissimum contra erit eandem omnino concedere; quapropter nobis hic inquirere incumbit quousque unicuique haec libertas salva reipublicae pace salvoque summarum potestatum iure potest & debet concedi, quod hic, ut in initio Cap. XVI monui, praecipuum meum intentum fuit.

11. Ex fundamentis reipublicae supra explicatis evidentissime sequitur finem eius ultimum non esse dominari nec homines metu retinere & alterius iuris facere, sed contra unumquemque metu liberare ut secure quoad eius fieri potest vivat, hoc est ut ius suum naturale ad exsistendum & operandum absque suo & alterius damno optime retineat. 12. Non inquam finis reipublicae est homines ex rationalibus bestias vel auto-

to put citizens to death for the slightest reasons; but everyone would agree that this would be against sound reason. Because, then, they could not behave in that way without great danger to the State, we can say they have *not* absolute power to do such things, and therefore not absolute right, since, as we have proved, the right of Sovereign Powers is bounded by their actual power.

8. If, then, no one *can* surrender his freedom to judge and opine as he chooses, each man being the master of his thoughts by the greatest right of nature, we must conclude that it is not possible in a State, without most unfortunate consequences, to try to make men, with their differing and incompatible opinions, say nothing but what is prescribed by the Supreme Power. For even the most prudent men, still less the ordinary people, cannot keep silent. 9. It is a failing common to humans to confide their opinions to others even when silence is plainly desirable. That State, then, is a most oppressive one in which individual liberty of speech and teaching is denied, and that is a temperately managed one in which it is allowed. 10. I am in no way denying that words can be as treasonable as deeds, so that although it is impossible to deprive subjects entirely of such liberty, it would be most damaging to allow it entirely. We must therefore inquire how far it can and ought to be granted without jeopardising the safety of the State or infringing the right of the Supreme Power—the question which, as I gave notice at the beginning of Ch. XVI, was to be my chief concern in this treatise.

11. From the origination of the State as expounded earlier it follows quite clearly that its ultimate purpose is not domination, not to repress men through fear, or to put them under an authority other than their own; but the very opposite, namely, to free them from fear by enabling them to live as safely as possible, or, in other words, to provide the way in which each may best retain his right to exist and act, i.e. without hurt either to himself or to others. 12. It is certainly not the purpose of the State to change men from rational

mata facere, sed contra ut eorum mens & corpus tuto suis functionibus fungantur & ipsi libera ratione utantur & ne odio ira vel dolo certent nec animo iniquo invicem ferantur. Finis ergo reipublicae revera libertas est.

13. Porro ad formandam rempublicam hoc unum necesse fuisse vidimus, nempe ut omnis decretandi potestas penes omnes vel aliquot vel penes unum esset. Nam quando quidem liberum hominum iudicium varium admodum est & unusquisque solus omnia scire putat, nec fieri potest ut omnes aeque eadem sentiant & uno ore loquantur, pacifice vivere non poterant nisi unusquisque iure agendi ex solo decreto suae mentis cederet. 14. Iure igitur agendi ex proprio decreto unusquisque tantum cessit, non autem ratiocinandi & iudicandi; adeoque salvo summarum potestatum iure nemo quidem contra earum decretum agere potest, at omnino sentire & iudicare & consequenter etiam dicere, modo simpliciter tantum dicat vel doceat & sola ratione non autem dolo ira odio, nec animo aliquid in rempublicam ex auctoritate sui decreti introducendi, defendat. 15. Ex. gr. si quis legem aliquam sanae rationi repugnare ostendit & propterea eandem abrogandam esse censet, si simul suam sententiam iudicio summae potestatis (cuius tantum est leges condere & abrogare) summittit & nihil interim contra illius legis praescriptum agit, bene sane de republica meretur ut optimus quisque civis. Sed si contra id faciat ad magistratum iniquitatis accusandum & vulgo odiosum reddendum vel seditiose studeat invito magistratu legem illam abrogare, omnino perturbator est & rebellis.

16. Videmus itaque qua ratione unusquisque, salvo iure & auctoritate summarum potestatum, hoc est salva reipublicae

beings into beasts or puppets, but to make it possible for them to use their mental and bodily capacities safely and their reason freely, and to keep them from the conflicts that come from hatred, anger and perfidy, and from behaving unfairly to one another. The real purpose of the State is freedom.

13. We also saw earlier that the one indispensable requisite for the formation of a State was that the power of decision should be wholly vested in all the citizens collectively, or in a few, or in one only, the reasons being that the opinions of free men differ considerably, that everyone supposes himself alone to be competent in all matters, that it is impossible for all men to think and speak in the same way, and consequently that they would not be able to live together peacefully unless everyone surrendered his right to *behave* by nothing but his own judgment. 14. It is this right only that each surrendered, not the right of reasoning and forming his own judgment. In consequence, while no man, consistently with the right of the Supreme Power, can *act* contrary to the latter's decree, he may surely form his own judgments and utter them, provided he does so sincerely, and defends them in a purely rational way, not with deceit, anger or hatred, or with the intention of introducing any change in the State on his own authority. 15. Suppose, for example, that someone proves that a particular law is contrary to sound reason, and accordingly believes that it should be abrogated: if nevertheless he submits his opinion to the decision of the Supreme Power (who alone has the right to enact and abrogate laws), and in the meantime does nothing contrary to that law, he deserves well of the State, as all the best citizens do. But if instead his motive is to accuse the magistrates of injustice and to rouse the hate of the populace against them, or if he sets himself to get the law abrogated against their will, he is nothing but an agitator and a rebel.

16. The condition under which, then, each man may say and teach what he thinks without detriment to the right of the Supreme Power, i.e. to the peace of the State, is that he leave

pace, ea quae sentit dicere & docere potest, nempe si decretum omnium rerum agendarum iisdem relinquat & nihil contra earum decretum agat, etiamsi saepe contra id quod bonum iudicat & palam sentit agere debeat; quod quidem salva iustitia & pietate facere potest, immo debet si se iustum & pium praestare vult. 17. Nam, ut iam ostendimus, iustitia a solo summarum potestatum decreto pendet, adeoque nemo nisi qui secundum earum recepta decreta vivit iustus esse potest. Pietas autem (per ea quae in praecedente Capite ostendimus) summa est quae circa pacem & tranquillitatem reipublicae exercetur; atqui haec conservari non potest si unicuique ex suo mentis arbitrio vivendum esset; adeoque impium etiam est ex suo arbitrio aliquid contra decretum summae potestatis cuius subditus est facere, quando quidem si hoc unicuique liceret imperii ruina inde necessario sequeretur. 18. Quin immo nihil contra decretum & dictamen propriae rationis agere potest quamdiu iuxta decreta summae potestatis agit; ipsa enim ratione suadente omnino decrevit ius suum vivendi ex proprio suo iudicio in eandem transferre. 19. Atqui hoc ipsa etiam praxi confirmare possumus; in conciliis namque tam summarum quam minorum potestatum raro aliquid fit ex communi omnium membrorum suffragio, et tamen omnia ex communi omnium decreto, tam scilicet eorum qui *contra* quam qui *pro* suffragium tulerunt, fiunt.

20. Sed ad meum propositum revertor. Qua ratione unusquisque iudicii libertate salvo iure summarum potestatum iure uti potest ex fundamentis reipublicae vidimus. At ex iis non minus facile determinare possumus quaenam opiniones in republica seditiosae sint, eae nimirum quae simul ac ponuntur pactum quo unusquisque iure agendi ex proprio suo arbitrio cessit tollitur. 21. Ex. gr. si quis sentiat summam potestatem sui iuris non esse, vel neminem promissis stare debere vel oportere unumquemque ex suo arbitrio vivere & alia huiusmodi

to the public authorities the right to decide about all matters of external conduct and do nothing contrary to their decree, even if he is thereby obliged to act contrary to what he thinks and publicly says to be good. Not only can he do this without detriment to justice and moral duty, but he ought to do it if he wishes to prove his own justice and moral goodness; 17. for, as I argued earlier, justice depends on the will of the Supreme Power alone, so that no one can be just unless he lives in accordance with that will so far as it is made known. As for moral duty, the highest form of it is (for the reasons given in the preceding chapter) that which makes for the peace of the State. Yet peace cannot be preserved if each man is to live as he pleases. It is therefore immoral for a man to do anything contrary to the will of the Supreme Power of which he is a subject, for if this were allowed to each subject the State would inevitably collapse. 18. Moreover, so long as he acts in accordance with the decrees of his Supreme Power he cannot act contrary to the decrees of his own reason, for it was through his reason that he resolved to transfer to a Supreme Power his right of living by his own judgment. 19. That there has been such a transference is confirmed by experience, for although in assemblies, sovereign as well as subordinate, it is rare for anything to be done by the unanimous vote of the members everything is done in the name of all, of those who have voted against it as well as of those who have voted for it.

20. To return to my main question. We have seen that the respect in which freedom of judgment can be exercised without prejudice to the rights of the Supreme Power follows from the very *raison d'être* of the State. From this same ground we may with equal ease also deduce what opinions are seditious, namely, those that have only to be expressed to be seen at once to involve the destruction of the compact by which everybody surrendered his right to act as he pleases. 21. For example, if anyone should hold the view that the Supreme Power does not possess absolute right, or that nobody is obliged to keep his promises, or that everyone ought to live by his

quae praedicto pacto directe repugnant, is seditiosus est, non tam quidem propter iudicium & opinionem quam propter factum quod talia iudicia involvunt, videlicet quia eo ipso quod tale quid sentit fidem summae potestati tacite vel expresse datam solvit; ac proinde ceterae opiniones quae actum non involvunt, nempe ruptionem pacti vindictam iram &c., seditiosae non sunt, nisi forte in republica aliqua ratione corrupta, ubi scilicet superstitiosi & ambitiosi qui ingenuos ferre nequeunt ad tantam nominis famam pervenerunt ut apud plebem plus valeat eorum quam summarum potestatum auctoritas.

23. Quod si denique ad hoc etiam attendamus quod fides uniuscuiusque erga rempublicam sicuti erga Deum ex solis operibus cognosci potest, nempe ex caritate erga proximum, nequaquam dubitare poterimus quin optima respublica unicuique eandem philosophandi libertatem concedat quam fidem unicuique concedere ostendimus. 24. Equidem fateor ex tali libertate incommoda quaedam aliquando oriri, verum quid umquam tam sapienter institutum fuit ut nihil inde incommodi oriri potuerit? Qui omnia legibus determinare vult vitia irritabit potius quam corriget. Quae prohiberi nequeunt necessario concedenda sunt, tametsi inde saepe damnum sequatur. 25. Quot enim mala ex luxu invidia avaritia ebrietate & aliis similibus oriuntur? Feruntur tamen haec quia imperio legum prohiberi nequeunt quamvis revera vitia sint. Quare multo magis iudicii libertas concedi debet quae profecto virtus est nec opprimi potest. 26. Adde quod nulla ex eadem incommoda oriuntur quae non possint (ut statim ostendam) auctoritate magistratuum vitari; ut iam taceam quod haec libertas apprime necessaria est ad scientias & artes promovendum, nam hae ab iis tantum felici cum successu coluntur qui iudicium liberum & minime praeoccupatum habent.

27. At ponatur hanc libertatem opprimi & homines ita

own judgment, or any other view directly contrary to the compact, such a person is seditious; not however so much because he has a view of his own as because of the practical implication of a view *of that kind*, namely, that his holding any *such* view breaks the promise of loyalty he has given, whether expressly or tacitly, to the Supreme Power. On the other hand, opinions that do not involve action, or the breaking of the compact, or revenge or anger, are not seditious, except perhaps in a State that is corrupt in some way, such as having in it superstitious and ambitious men who are unable to tolerate generous minds, and have gained so great a reputation that they have more authority over the masses than the Supreme Power has.

23. If now we bear in mind that fidelity to the State, like fidelity to God, can be known only by external behaviour, namely, by love towards one's neighbour, we shall find it indubitable that the best kind of State should grant to everyone the same freedom in philosophy which, as I argued earlier, it should grant in religious belief. 24. I admit that such freedom can on occasion cause inconvenience. But what human system has ever been so skilfully devised that no inconvenience could spring from it? Anyone who wants to settle everything by laws will provoke vices rather than correct them. What cannot be forbidden must be allowed, even if harm often results. 25. How many evils spring from debauchery, envy, greed, drunkenness and the like! Yet these are borne, although undoubtedly wicked, because laws cannot deal with them. How much more, then, should freedom of opinion be allowed, being not a vice but a virtue, and not capable of being suppressed! 26. Besides, the inconveniences that spring from it can all be avoided (as I shall show presently) by the authority of the magistrates; and I may note in passing that such liberty is utterly necessary for the advancement of the arts and sciences, since these can only be cultivated with good result by those whose judgment is free and unprejudiced.

27. Suppose this freedom could be suppressed and men be

retineri posse ut nihil muttire audeant nisi ex praescripto summarum potestatum; hoc profecto numquam fiet ut nihil etiam nisi quid ipsae velint cogitent. Atque adeo necessario sequeretur ut homines cottidie aliud sentirent aliud loquerentur, & consequenter ut fides in republica apprime necessaria corrumperetur, & abominanda adulatio & perfidia foverentur, unde doli & omnium bonarum artium corruptio. 28. Verum longe abest ut id fieri possit ut omnes scilicet praefinito loquantur, sed contra quo magis libertas loquendi hominibus adimi curatur eo contumacius contra nituntur, non quidem avari adulatores & reliqui impotentes animi quorum summa salus est nummos in arca contemplari & ventres distentos habere, sed ii quos bona educatio morum integritas & virtus liberiores fecit. 29. Ita homines plerumque constituti sunt ut nihil magis impatienter ferant quam quod opiniones quas veras esse credunt pro crimine habeantur, & quod ipsis sceleri reputetur id quod ipsos ad pietatem erga Deum & homines movet, ex quo fit ut leges detestari & quidvis in magistratum audeant, nec turpe sed honestissimum putent seditiones hac de causa movere & quodvis facinus temptare. 30. Cum itaque humanam naturam sic comparatam esse constet, sequitur leges quae de opinionibus conduntur non scelestos sed ingenuos respicere, nec ad malignos coercendum sed potius ad honestos irritandum condi, nec sine magno imperii periculo defendi posse. 31. Adde quod tales leges inutiles omnino sunt, nam qui opiniones quae legibus damnatae sunt sanas esse credent legibus parere non poterunt, qui contra easdem tamquam falsas reiciunt leges quibus hae damnantur tamquam privilegia recipiunt & iisdem ita triumphant ut magistratus easdem postea etsi velit abrogare non valeat. 32....Et denique quot schismata in Ecclesia ex hoc plerumque orta sunt, quod magistatus doctorum con-

kept from daring to murmur anything but what the Supreme Power prescribes.

Even so they could by no means be kept also from *thinking* only what the Supreme Power wills. The inevitable result would be that men would daily think in one way and speak in another. The trust that is utterly necessary in a State would thus be destroyed, and despicable fawning and bad faith would be encouraged, resulting in all sorts of deception and the decay of all honest occupations. 28. But it is quite impossible to make all men speak to order: the greater the measures taken to deprive them of freedom of speech, the more rebellious do they become—not, of course, the avaricious, the flatterers and the rest of the weakminded, whose chief welfare is to gloat over the coins in their coffers and to fill their bellies, but those men to whom a good upbringing, moral integrity and mental strength have given some degree of independence of mind. 29. It is the very nature of most men to find nothing more intolerable than the branding as crimes of opinions they believe to be true, or as wicked of what moves them to be dutiful to God and their fellow-men. Consequently, they execrate the laws and, believing that whatever they do against the magistrates is not wrong but eminently right, foment revolts and commit themselves to all sorts of evil deeds. 30. Human nature being, then, notoriously so constituted, laws against opinions have in view not wicked men but the honourable ones, are framed not to restrain the bad but rather to anger the good, and cannot be maintained without great danger to the State. 31. Moreover, they are ineffective; for, on the one hand, those who believe that the opinions forbidden by the laws are sound will not be able to obey the laws, and on the other hand, those who reject such opinions as false will regard the laws that forbid them as marks of favour to themselves, and will be so delighted with them that the magistrates will not be able to abrogate them if they should ever wish to do so. 32....Bear in mind also how many schisms have arisen in the Church usually because magistrates

troversias legibus dirimere voluerunt. Nam ni homines spe tenerentur leges & magistratum ad se trahendi & de suis adversariis communi vulgi applausu triumphandi & honores adipiscendi, numquam tam iniquo animo certarent nec tantus furor eorum mentes agitaret.

33. Atque haec non tantum ratio sed etiam experientia cottidianis exemplis docet, nempe similes leges quibus scilicet imperatur quid unicuique credendum sit et contra hanc aut illam opinionem aliquid dicere vel scribere prohibetur, saepe institutas fuisse ad largiendum vel potius cedendum eorum ira qui libera ingenia ferre nequeunt & torva quadam auctoritate seditiosae plebis devotionem facile in rabiem mutare & in quos volunt instigare possunt. 34. At quanto satius foret vulgi iram & furorem cohibere quam leges inutiles statuere quae violari non possunt nisi ab iis qui virtutes & artes amant, & rempublicam in tantam angustiam redigere ut viros ingenuos sustinere non possit. 35. Quid enim maius reipublicae malum excogitare potest quam quod viri honesti, quia diversa sentiunt & simulare nesciunt, tamquam improbi in exsilium mittantur? Quid inquam magis perniciosum quam quod homines ob nullum scelus neque facinus sed quia liberalis ingenii sunt pro hostibus habeantur & ad necem ducantur, & quod catasta, malorum formido, pulcherrimum fiat theatrum ad summum tolerantiae & virtutis exemplum cum insigni maiestatis opprobrio ostentandum? 36. Qui enim se honestos norunt mortem ut scelesti non timent nec supplicium deprecantur; eorum quippe animus nulla turpis facti paenitentia angitur, sed contra honestum non supplicium putant pro bona causa mori & pro libertate gloriosum. Quid ergo talium nece exempli statuitur cuius causam inertes & animo impotentes ignorant, seditiosi oderunt, & honesti amant? Nemo sane ex eadem exemplum capere potest nisi ad imitandum vel saltem ad adulandum.

have set themselves to end the disputes of the learned by legal pressure. If men did not have the hope of drawing the law and the magistracy to their side, of triumphing over their adversaries with the applause of the common people, and of thereby climbing into office themselves, they would not conduct their disputes as unfairly and furiously as they do.

33. Experience supports reason by supplying evidence daily that laws which prescribe either what is to be believed or what is not to be uttered in speech or writing have often been instituted as a sop, or rather as a surrender, to the wrath of those who cannot tolerate men of independent mind and, unscrupulous in their influence, easily whip up the religious passion of the factious populace into a mad rage, and turn this against whom they please. 34. How much better it would be to restrain the anger and wildness of the mob instead of enacting useless laws which can be broken only by men that love the things of the mind, and reducing the State to the point where it cannot tolerate those who are frankly upright! 35. What greater harm to the State is conceivable than that good men should be banished from it as wicked on the ground that they think differently from the rest and cannot pretend that they do not? Whatever could be more ruinous than that men should be treated as enemies and put to death not for any crime or wicked deed but because they freely do their own thinking; that the scaffold, the terror of evildoers, should be made the pompous stage on which the greatest embodiments of virtue and tolerance are exhibited in disgrace at the high behest of the Supreme Power? 36. Unlike the wicked, those who have a good conscience do not fear death, and do not beg for mercy; not being tormented by repentance for an evil deed they count it not a punishment but an honour to die for a good cause, a matter of just pride to die for freedom. What sort of example is set by the killing of such men, whose cause is unknown to the idle and weakminded, hated by the factious, and loved by the good? The only lesson that can be drawn is that such men are to be imitated, or at any rate to be held in deep respect.

37. Ne itaque assentatio sed ut fides in pretio sit, & ut summae potestates imperium optime retineant nec seditiosis cedere cogantur, iudicii libertas necessario concedenda est & homines ita regendi sunt ut quamvis diversa & contraria palam sentiant concorditer tamen vivant. Nec dubitare possumus quin haec ratio imperandi optima sit & minora patiatur incommoda, quando quidem cum hominum natura maxime convenit.

38. In imperio enim democratico (quod maxime ad statum naturalem accedit) omnes pacisci ostendimus ex communi decreto agere at non iudicare & ratiocinari, hoc est quia omnes homines non possunt aeque eadem sentire, pacti sunt ut id vim decreti haberet quod plurima haberet suffragia, retinendo interim auctoritatem eadem ubi meliora viderint abrogandi. Quo igitur hominibus libertas iudicandi minus conceditur eo a statu maxime naturali magis receditur & consequenter violentius regnatur.

39. Ut autem porro constet ex hac libertate nulla oriri incommoda quae non possint sola summae potestatis auctoritate vitari, & hac sola homines etsi palam contraria sentientes facile retineri ne invicem laedant, exempla praesto sunt, nec opus mihi est ea longe petere. 40. Urbs Amstelodamum exemplo sit, quae tantum cum suo incremento & omnium nationum admiratione huius libertatis fructus experitur. In hac enim florentissima republica & urbe praestantissima omnes cuiuscumque nationis & sectae homines summa cum concordia vivunt, & ut alicui bona sua credant id tantum scire curant num dives an pauper sit & num bona fide an dolo solitus sit agere. Ceterum religio vel secta nihil eos movet, quia haec coram iudice ad iustificandam vel damnandam causam nihil iuvat; & nulla omnino tam odiosa secta est cuius sectarii (modo neminem laedant & suum unicuique tribuant honesteque

37. If not flattery but trustworthiness is to be esteemed, and the Supreme Power is to maintain its position well, not being compelled to give way to the factious, it is necessary to allow freedom of thought, and so to govern that subjects may live together in concord, however different and even opposed their expressed opinions may be. This is undoubtedly the best way of governing, and the least liable to inconveniences, for it is the one most suited to human nature.

38. In a democratic State—the one that comes nearest to man's natural condition—what all men have pledged themselves to do is, as I have shown, to *act*, not to reason and opine, in accordance with the collective decree; i.e. because it is impossible for all of them to come to the same conclusions, they have agreed that what is approved by the majority shall have the force of law, while retaining the right to abrogate it when they come to think of anything that seems better. Therefore, the less a State allows freedom of thought, the further it is from the perfectly natural condition of men, and the more oppressive will be its rule.

39. That such freedom does not give rise to any inconveniences that cannot be avoided by the mere authority of the Supreme Power, and that by this alone men can easily be prevented, though openly holding incompatible views, from injuring one another, can be proved by actual instances. I do not need to look far for one. 40. Let the city of Amsterdam suffice. It has enjoyed the fruits of that freedom while expanding its prosperity and exciting the wonder of all nations. In this flourishing State, this outstanding city, people of every nation and sect live together in complete concord. For instance, when they are considering whom to entrust with their goods, all that they take into account is whether the persons in view are rich or poor, and whether they habitually act in good or in bad faith. What religion or sect they belong to is ignored, as being irrelevant to any possible action in a court of law. There is no sect so detested that its followers are not protected by the authority and arm of the State, provided only that they

vivant) publica magistratuum auctoritate & praesidio non protegantur. 41. Contra cum olim Remonstrantium & Contraremonstrantium controversia de religione * a politicis & ordinibus provinciarum agitari incepit tandem in schisma abiit, & multis tum exemplis constitit leges quae de religione conduntur ad dirimendas scilicet controversias homines magis irritare quam corrigere, alios deinde infinitam ex iisdem licentiam sumere; praeterea schismata non oriri ex magno veritatis studio (fonte scilicet comitatis & mansuetudinis) sed ex magna libidine regnandi. 42. Ex quibus luce meridiana clarius constat eos potius schismaticos esse qui aliorum scripta damnant & vulgum petulantem in scriptores seditiose instigant quam scriptores ipsi qui plerumque doctis tantum scribunt & solam rationem in auxilium vocant; deinde eos revera perturbatores esse qui in libera republica libertatem iudicii quae non potest opprimi tollere tamen volunt.

43. His ostendimus I. impossibile esse libertatem hominibus dicendi ea quae sentiunt adimere; II. hanc libertatem salvo iure & auctoritate summarum potestatum unicuique concedi, & eandem unumquemque servare posse salvo eodem iure si nullam inde licentiam sumat ad aliquid in rempublicam tamquam ius introducendum vel aliquid contra receptas leges agendum; III. hanc eandem libertatem unumquemque habere posse servata reipublicae pace, & nulla ex eadem incommoda oriri quae facile coerceri non possint; IV. eandem salva etiam pietate unumquemque habere posse; V. leges quae de rebus speculativis conduntur inutiles omnino esse. 44. VI. Denique ostendimus hanc libertatem non tantum servata reipublicae pace pietate & summarum potestatum iure posse, sed ad haec omnia conservandum etiam debere concedi. Nam ubi ex adverso eandem hominibus adimere laboratur & discrepantium opiniones non autem animi, qui soli peccare possunt, in iudicium

---

* A dispute among Dutch Protestants about Calvin's doctrine of predestination. The Remonstrants had issued a statement against it in 1610. See above, p. *xvi*.

injure nobody, give to each man his due, and live uprightly. 41. It was not so during the religious controversy between the Remonstrants and Counter-Remonstrants *: the statesmen and the Provincial Estates took part in the dispute, which ended in a schism, the affair providing many instances which prove that laws aimed at dealing with religious disputes provoke men rather than correct them, that some men exploit such laws with boundless license, and that schisms arise not from a specially strong zeal for truth (this being a source of kindness and gentleness) but from a lust for domination. 42. From which it is plainer than the noonday sun that it is those who condemn the writings of others, and stir up the wanton mob against the writers, who are the schismatics, rather than the writers themselves, who usually address themselves only to the learned and appeal only to reason; and that they are the real disturbers of the peace who, in a free State, try to suppress freedom of thought, which cannot in fact be suppressed.

43. The conclusions I have argued are these. I. It is impossible to take away from men the freedom to say what they think. II. This freedom can be granted to every man without prejudice to the right and authority of the Supreme Power, and can be retained by every man provided he does not use it as a warrant for introducing into the community anything that is in effect a new law, or for doing anything against the acknowledged laws. III. This same freedom can be possessed by everybody without disturbing the peace of the State, and no inconveniences can follow from it that cannot easily be held in check. IV. It can be possessed by everybody without prejudice to piety. V. Laws about matters of speculation are quite useless. 44. VI. Such freedom *can* in fact be innocuous to the peace of the State, piety, and the right of the Supreme Power, and *ought* to be granted in order to preserve all these.

Where, on the contrary, the attempt is made to take away such freedom, and dissenters are brought to trial for their opinions—not for their intentions, which alone are capable of being morally wrong—good men are subjected to punish-

vocantur, ibi in honestos exempla eduntur, quae potius martyria videntur quaeque reliquos magis irritant & ad misericordiam si non ad vindictam plus movent quam terrent. 45. Bonae deinde artes & fides corrumpuntur, adulatores & perfidi foventur, & adversarii triumphant quod eorum irae concessum sit quodque imperium tenentes suae doctrinae cuius interpretes habentur sectatores fecerint, ex quo fit ut eorum auctoritatem & ius usurpare audeant, nec iactare erubescant se a Deo immediate electos & sua decreta divina, summarum autem potestatum contra humana esse quae propterea divinis, hoc est suis decretis, ut cedant volunt; quae omnia nemo ignorare potest reipublicae saluti omnino repugnare. 46. Quapropter hic, ut supra Cap. XVIII concludimus, nihil reipublicae tutius quam ut pietas & religio in solo caritatis & aequitatis exercitio comprehendatur, & ius summarum potestatum tam circa sacra quam profana ad actiones tantum referatur, ceterum unicuique & sentire quae velit & quae sentiat dicere concedatur.

47. His quae in hoc tractatu agere constitueram absolvi. Superest tantum expresse monere me nihil in eo scripsisse quod non libentissime examini & iudicio summarum potestatum patriae meae subiciam; nam si quid horum quae dixi patriis legibus repugnare vel communi saluti obesse iudicabunt, id ego indictum volo. Scio me hominem esse & errare potuisse. Ne autem errarem sedulo curavi & apprime ut quicquid scriberem legibus patriae pietati bonisque moribus omnino responderet.

FINIS

ments that seem more like martyrdoms, affecting other men less with fear than with compassion, or even with the spirit of revenge. 45. Liberal pursuits and good faith thereby deteriorate, and fawners and traitors are encouraged. The opponents of freedom exult because their indignation has been yielded to, also because they have converted the Supreme Power to the doctrines of which they are the recognised spokesmen; and on this ground they usurp its authority, shamelessly boasting that they themselves were directly appointed by God and that their judgments are divine while those of the Supreme Power are merely human, and accordingly claim that the latter should give way to the former. All these consequences are obviously contrary to the welfare of the State. 46. We must conclude, then, that the safety of the State is best secured by taking piety or religion to mean only the practice of charity and equity, and by restricting the right of the Supreme Power, in sacred as in secular affairs, to overt actions, leaving to every individual the liberty to think what he wills and to say what he thinks.

47. Here I finish what I set out to do in this treatise. Nothing remains for me to say except that I have written nothing but what I gladly submit to the scrutiny and judgement of my country's Supreme Power. If anything I have said is judged by the Supreme Power to be contrary to the country's laws or to be an obstacle to the public welfare, I am willing to withdraw it publicly. I know that I am but human, and therefore may have erred; but to avoid erring, I have made it my special care to write only what is in complete harmony with my country's laws, with piety, and with sound morals.

TRACTATUS POLITICUS

in quo demonstratur
quomodo societas ubi imperium monarchicum locum habet
sicut ut ea ubi optimi imperant
debet institui ne in tyrannidem labatur
& ut pax libertasque civium inviolata maneat

A POLITICAL TREATISE

in which it is proved
how monarchies and aristocracies are to be constituted
in order to avoid falling into tyranny
and to preserve peace and the freedom of the citizens

CAP. I

1. Adfectus quibus conflictamur concipiunt philosophi veluti vitia in quae homines sua culpa labuntur, quos propterea ridere flere carpere vel (qui sanctiores videri volunt) detestari solent. Sic ergo se rem divinam facere & sapientiae culmen attingere credunt quando humanam naturam quae nullibi est multis modis laudare, & eam quae revera est dictis lacessere norunt. Homines namque non ut sunt sed ut eosdem esse vellent concipiunt, unde factum est ut plerumque pro Ethica satiram scripserint, & ut numquam Politicam conceperint quae possit ad usum revocari sed quae pro chimaera haberetur, vel quae in Utopia vel in illo poetarum aureo saeculo ubi scilicet minime necesse erat institui potuisset. Cum igitur omnium scientiarum quae usum habent tum maxime politices theoria ab ipsius praxi discrepare creditur, & regendae reipublicae nulli minus idonei aestimantur quam theoretici seu philosophi.

2. At politici contra hominibus insidiari quam consulere creduntur, & potius callidi quam sapientes aestimantur. Docuit nimirum eosdem experientia vitia fore donec homines. Humanam igitur malitiam praevenire dum student, idque iis artibus quas experientia longo usu docuit & quas homines magis metu quam ratione ducti exercere solent, religioni adversari videntur, theologis praecipue, qui credunt summas potestates debere negotia publica tractare secundum easdem pietatis regulas quibus vir privatus tenetur. Ipsos tamen politicos multo felicius de rebus politicis scripsisse quam philosophos dubitari non pot-

CH. I. POLITICAL ORDER AS THE CONTROL OF HUMAN PASSIONS

1. Philosophers think of the passions that disturb us as vices into which we fall through our own fault, and on this ground deride, deplore or censure them; and those who wish to seem holier than other men invoke divine curses on them. They think that they are carrying out a sacred task, and have reached the peak of human wisdom, when they have learned to lavish praises on a human nature that does not exist and to inveigh against the one that does. They are thinking of men not as they are but as they themselves would like them to be. Hence instead of ethics they have usually written satire, and have never devised a political theory that could be put into practice, but a merely imaginary sort that might be set up in Utopia or in the golden age sung of by the poets, where, of course, it would be least needed. It is therefore generally accepted that the discrepancy between theory and practice that marks all applied sciences is greatest in the science of politics, and that nobody is less fit to govern a State than a philosopher.

2. Statesmen, in their turn, are thought rather to work against than for the interest of the people, and to be more cunning than wise. They, of course, have learned from experience that there will be vices as long as there are men. Because of their concern to forestall human wickedness by using devices taught by long practice and characteristic of men moved more by fear than reason, they are supposed to be hostile to religion, especially by theologians, who believe that rulers are subject to the very same rules of duty in their handling of public affairs as private citizens are in theirs. Nevertheless, statesmen have undoubtedly written more aptly than philo-

est, nam quoniam experientiam magistram habuerunt nihil docuerunt quod ab usu remotum esset.

4. Cum igitur animum ad Politicam applicuerim, nihil quod novum vel inauditum est sed tantum ea quae cum praxi optime conveniunt certa & indubitata ratione demonstrare, aut ex ipsa humanae naturae condicione deducere, intendi; & ut ea quae ad hanc scientiam spectant eadem animi libertate qua res mathematicas solemus inquirerem, sedulo curavi humanas actiones non ridere non lugere neque detestari sed intellegere, atque adeo humanos adfectus, ut sunt amor odium ira invidia gloria misericordia & reliquae animi commotiones, non ut humanae naturae vitia sed ut proprietates contemplatus sum quae ad ipsam ita pertinent ut ad naturam aëris aestus frigus tempestas tonitru & alia huiusmodi, quae tametsi incommoda sunt necessaria tamen sunt certasque habent causas per quas eorum naturam intellegere conamur, & mens eorum vera contemplatione aeque gaudet ac earum rerum cognitione quae sensibus gratae sunt.

5. Est enim hoc certum, & in nostra *Ethica* * verum esse demonstravimus, homines necessario adfectibus esse obnoxios & ita constitutos esse ut eorum quibus male est misereantur & quibus bene est invideant, & ut ad vindictam magis quam ad misericordiam sint proni, & praeterea unumquemque appetere ut reliqui ex ipsius ingenio vivant & ut probent quod ipse probat & quod ipse repudiat repudient; unde fit ut, cum omnes pariter appetant primi esse, in contentiones veniant & quantum possunt nitantur se invicem opprimere, & qui victor evadit magis glorietur quod alteri obfuit quam quod sibi profuit. Et quamvis omnes persuasi sint religionem contra docere ut unusquisque proximum tamquam se ipsum amet, hoc est ut ius alterius perinde ac suum defendat, hanc tamen persuasionem in adfectus parum posse ostendimus. Valet quidem in articulo mortis quando scilicet morbus ipsos adfectus

---

* On this paragraph see especially *Ethics* IV, Prop. 4 coroll.; Appendix to IV; V, Prop. 42 note.

sophers on political matters, for, experience being their teacher, they have recommended nothing out of touch with practice.

4. My aim in the consideration of politics is not to publish a novel theory but to seek truths of practical value, and to establish them by precise and cogent demonstration, starting from human nature as it is; and in order to do so with the same detachment in this field as is customary in mathematics, I have tried hard not to deride, lament or execrate human actions, but simply to understand them, viewing passions such as love, hatred, anger, envy, ambition and pity not as vices of our nature but as properties that belong to it in the same way that heat, cold, storm, thunder and the like belong to the nature of the atmosphere. Although they are troublesome, they are necessarily what they are, having fixed causes by means of which we try to understand them; and in understanding them truly the mind finds pleasure, just as it does in the knowledge of things that gratify the senses.

5. It is certain (I have proved it in my *Ethics* *) that human beings are subject to passions necessarily; in particular, that they are so constituted as to pity the unfortunate, envy the fortunate, and be more prone to revenge than mercy, and that everyone wants everybody else to live as he would like them to do, approve what he approves and reject what he rejects. All of them alike trying to be foremost, they come into conflict: they do their best to overthrow one another, and whoever is victor takes more pride in the harm he has inflicted than in the benefit he has got. Even though all of them may believe that this is contrary to the religious requirement that everyone should love his neighbour as himself (i.e. should guard the right of another as he would his own), this belief, I have argued, has scarcely any power over the passions. It is, indeed, strong in our dying moments, when disease has overcome even the

vicit & homo segnis iacet, vel in templis ubi homines nullum exercent commercium, at minime in foro vel in aula ubi maxime necesse esset. Ostendimus praeterea rationem multum quidem posse adfectus coercere & moderari, sed simul vidimus viam quam ipsa ratio docet perarduam esse, ita ut qui sibi persuadent posse multitudinem vel qui publicis negotiis distrahuntur induci ut ex solo rationis praescripto vivant saeculum poetarum aureum seu fabulam somnient.

6. Imperium igitur cuius salus ab alicuius fide pendet, & cuius negotia non possunt recte curari nisi ii qui eadem tractant fide velint agere, minime stabile erit; sed ut permanere possit res eius publicae ita ordinandae sunt ut qui easdem administrant, sive ratione ducantur sive adfectu, induci nequeant ut male fidi sint seu prave agant. Nec ad imperii securitatem refert quo animo homines inducantur ad res recte administrandum, modo res recte administrentur; animi enim libertas seu fortitudo privata virtus est, at imperii virtus securitas.

7. Denique quia omnes homines, sive barbari sive culti sint, consuetudines ubique iungunt & statum aliquem civilem formant; ideo imperii causas & fundamenta naturalia non ex rationis documentis petenda sed ex hominum communi natura seu condicione deducenda sunt, quod in sequenti Capite facere constitui.

CAP. II

2. Res quaecumque naturalis potest adaequate concipi sive exsistat sive non exsistat. Ut igitur rerum naturalium exsistendi principium sic earum in exsistendo perseverantia ex earum definitione non potest concludi. Nam earum essentia idealis eadem est postquam exsistere inceperunt quam antequam exsisterent...

passions and we lie impotent, and in church, where we are not doing anything to one another; it is at its weakest in law-court and palace, where the need of it, one would think, is the greatest. I argued also that reason can certainly do much to check and control the passions, but at the same time I made it clear that the way thereto enjoined by reason is a very difficult one, so that those who believe that either the general mass of the people or those who are harassed by public duties can be led to live under the guidance of reason alone, are dreaming of the poets' golden age or of some other fiction.

6. Any State, then, whose safety depends on anyone's good faith, and whose affairs cannot be conducted rightly unless those responsible are resolved to act in good faith, will scarcely be a stable one. In order to be capable of enduring, its public affairs must be so ordered that those who administer them, whether following reason or passion, cannot in practice be seduced into bad faith or wicked action. For a State's stability it does not matter what motive leads men to administer its affairs rightly, but only that they *be* administered rightly; for freedom or strength of character is a private virtue, the virtue of the State being stability.

7. Finally, since all men, whether savage or civilised, everywhere come together socially and form some sort of civil order, the causes and natural bases of the State are not to be looked for in the abstract principles of reason but are to be deduced from the nature or condition common to all mankind. This I shall do in the next chapter.

CH. II. RIGHT AND POWER, NATURAL AND POLITICAL

2. All natural things can be conceived adequately irrespective of whether they are existing or not. Neither their beginning nor their continuing to exist can be deduced from their definition, for the conceived essence is the same after they have begun to exist as before... The power requisite to bring

Eadem potentia qua indigent ut exsistere incipiant indigent ut exsistere pergant. Ex quo sequitur rerum naturalium potentiam qua exsistunt & consequenter qua operantur nullam aliam esse posse quam ipsam Dei aeternam potentiam. Nam si quae alia creata esset non posset se ipsam & consequenter neque res naturales conservare, sed ipsa etiam eadem potentia qua indigeret ut crearetur indigeret ut in exsistendo perseveraret.

3. Hinc igitur, quod scilicet rerum naturalium potentia qua exsistunt & operantur ipsissima Dei sit potentia, facile intellegimus quid ius naturae sit. Nam quoniam Deus ius ad omnia habet & ius Dei nihil aliud est quam ipsa Dei potentia quatenus haec absolute libera consideratur, hinc sequitur unamquamque rem naturalem tantum iuris ex natura habere quantum potentiae habet ad exsistendum & operandum....

4. Per ius itaque naturae intellego ipsas naturae leges seu regulas secundum quas omnia fiunt, hoc est ipsam naturae potentiam; atque adeo totius naturae & consequenter uniuscuiusque individui naturale ius eo usque se extendit quo eius potentia, & consequenter quicquid unusquisque homo ex legibus suae naturae agit id summo naturae iure agit, tantumque in naturam habet iuris quantum potentia valet.

5. Si igitur cum humana natura ita comparatum esset ut homines ex solo rationis praescripto viverent nec aliud conarentur, tum naturae ius, quatenus humani generis proprium esse consideratur, sola rationis potentia determinaretur. Sed homines magis caeca cupiditate quam ratione ducuntur, ac proinde hominum naturalis potentia sive ius non ratione sed quocumque appetitu quo ad agendum determinantur quoque se conservare conantur definiri debet. Equidem fateor cupiditates illas quae ex ratione non oriuntur non tam actiones quam passiones esse humanas. Verum quia hic de naturae universali potentia seu iure agimus, nullam hic agnoscere possumus differentiam inter cupiditates quae ex ratione & inter illas quae ex aliis causis in nobis ingenerantur, quando quidem tam hae quam illae effectus naturae sunt vimque naturalem explicant qua homo in suo esse perseverare conatur. Est enim homo,

them into existence is requisite to their continuing to exist. The power by which they exist, and consequently by which they act, cannot be anything else than the eternal power of God, for if it were a created power it could not preserve itself, and therefore could not preserve natural things—it would itself need for its continuing existence the power that was requisite for its creation.

3. Granted that the power in virtue of which natural things exist and act is none other than the power of God, it is easy to grasp what the right of nature is. Because God has the right to everything, and because His right is simply His power regarded as absolutely free, each natural thing has from nature as much right as it has power to exist and act...

4. Therefore I take the *right* of nature to be the very laws or rules of nature in accordance with which all things come to exist; in other words, the *power* of nature. The natural right of nature as a whole, and therefore of each thing within it, is co-extensive with its power. Consequently, whatever any human being does because of the laws of his own nature he does by the supreme right of nature, and has as much right over nature as he has effective power.

5. Now if human beings were so equipped as to live solely by what reason prescribes, never seeking anything else, the right of nature in its peculiarly human form would be bounded by the power of reason alone. Human beings, however, are led more by blind desire than by reason. Therefore their natural power or right is to be defined not by their reason but by whatever appetite moves them to act and to strive to preserve themselves. I admit that in the desires that do not spring from reason we are not so much active as passive; but since I am at present considering the power or right common to everything in nature, I cannot yet draw the distinction between desires that spring from reason and those that arise from other causes; all of them alike being natural effects, they express the natural force with which a man strives to maintain his own being. Whether led by reason or no, a man is a part of

sive sapiens sive ignarus sit, naturae pars, & id omne ex quo unusquisque ad agendum determinatur ad naturae potentiam referri debet, nempe quatenus haec per naturam huius aut illius hominis definiri potest. Nihil namque homo, seu ratione seu sola cupiditate ductus, agit nisi secundum leges & regulas naturae, hoc est ex naturae iure.

6. At plerique ignaros naturae ordinem magis perturbare quam sequi credunt & homines in natura veluti imperium in imperio concipiunt. Nam mentem humanam a nullis causis naturalibus statuunt produci sed a Deo immediate creari, a reliquis rebus adeo independentem ut absolutam habeat potestatem sese determinandi & ratione recte utendi. Sed experientia satis superque docet quod in nostra potestate non magis sit mentem sanam quam corpus sanum habere. Deinde quando quidem unaquaeque res quantum in se est suum esse conservare conatur, dubitare nequaquam possumus quin si aeque in nostra potestate esset tam ex rationis praescripto vivere quam caeca cupiditate duci, omnes ratione ducerentur & vitam sapienter instituerent, quod minime fit. Nam trahit sua quemque voluptas*....

7. ... Est namque libertas virtus seu perfectio. Quicquid igitur hominem impotentiae arguit id ad ipsius libertatem referri nequit. Quare homo minime potest dici liber propterea quod potest non exsistere vel quod potest non uti ratione, sed tantum quatenus potestatem habet exsistendi & operandi secundum humanae naturae leges. Quo igitur hominem magis liberum esse consideramus eo minus dicere possumus quod possit ratione non uti & mala prae bonis eligere; & ideo Deus, qui absolute liber exsistit intelligit & operatur, necessario etiam nempe ex suae naturae necessitate exsistit intelligit & operatur. Nam non dubium est quin Deus eadem qua exsistit libertate operetur. Ut igitur ex ipsius naturae necessitate exsistit, ex ipsius etiam naturae necessitate agit, hoc est libere absolute agit.

---

* Virg., *Ecl.* II, 65.

nature, so that everything that moves him to act is to be referred to the power of nature so far as this is specified in the nature of the rational or the irrational man. All that he does, whether moved by reason or by nothing but desire, is done according to the laws or rules of nature, i.e. by the right of nature.

6. It is generally believed, however, that uneducated men infringe the order of nature rather than conform to it, and that human beings are as it were a State within a State—that the human mind is not a product of natural causes but the direct creation of God, so independent of all other beings that it has an absolute power to determine itself and make a proper use of reason. But experience shows abundantly that to have a sound mind is no more within our power than to have a sound body. Also, since everything does its utmost to preserve its own being, if it were as much within our power to live by reason as by blind desire, we should have to infer that everybody would follow reason, conducting his life wisely; and this conclusion is not true in fact. Everybody is impelled by what he regards as pleasant....

7. ... Freedom is a virtue or perfection, so that anything that is a sign of weakness in a man cannot be attributed to his freedom. A man cannot be called free, then, on the ground that it is possible for him not to exist, or not to use reason, but only so far as he has in fact the power to exist and to behave in accordance with the laws of human nature. Therefore the freer we count a man to be, the less can we say that it is possible for him not to use reason and to prefer what is bad to what is good. God, who exists and understands and acts with perfect freedom, does so necessarily, i.e. by the necessity of His own nature. Undoubtedly He acts with the same freedom with which He exists, and as He exists by the necessity of His own nature, by the necessity of His own nature He also acts, i.e. He acts with perfect freedom.

8. Concludimus itaque in potestate uniuscuiusque hominis non esse ratione semper uti & in summo humanae libertatis fastigio esse.... Ex quibus sequitur ius & institutum naturae sub quo omnes nascuntur homines & maxima ex parte vivunt nihil nisi quod nemo cupit & quod nemo potest prohibere, non contentiones non odia non iram non dolos nec absolute aliquid quod appetitus suadet aversari....

9. Praeterea sequitur unumquemque tamdiu alterius esse iuris quamdiu sub alterius potestate est, & eatenus sui iuris quatenus vim omnem repellere, damnumque sibi illatum ex sui animi sententia vindicare, & absolute quatenus ex suo ingenio vivere potest. **10.** Is alterum sub potestate habet quem ligatum tenet, vel cui arma & media sese defendendi aut evadendi ademit, vel qui metum iniecit, vel quem sibi beneficio ita devinxit ut ei potius quam sibi morem gerere & potius ex ipsius quam ex sui animi sententia vivere velit. Qui primo vel secundo modo alterum in potestate habet eius tantum corpus non mentem tenet; tertio autem vel quarto, tam ipsius mentem quam corpus sui iuris fecit, sed non nisi durante metu vel spe, hac vero aut illo adempto manet alter sui iuris.

11. Iudicandi facultas eatenus etiam alterius iuris esse potest quatenus mens potest ab altero decipi; ex quo sequitur mentem eatenus sui iuris omnino esse quatenus recte uti potest ratione. Immo quia humana potentia non tam ex corporis robore quam ex mentis fortitudine aestimanda est, hinc sequitur illos maxime sui iuris esse qui maxime ratione pollent quique maxime eadem ducuntur; atque adeo hominem eatenus liberum omnino voco quatenus ratione ducitur, quia eatenus ex causis quae per solam eius naturam possunt adaequate intellegi ad agendum determinatur, tametsi ex iis necessario ad agendum determinetur; nam libertas (ut Art. 7 huius Cap. ostendimus) agendi necessitatem non tollit sed ponit.

8. It is not in the power of everybody, then, to be always using his reason, i.e. to be perfectly free... It follows that the right and law of nature, under which all men are born and for the most part live, forbids only what nobody can in fact desire or do: it does not keep us from strife, hatred, anger, deceit, or anything at all to which our appetite prompts us....

9. It follows also that a man is under the right of another as long as he is under the other's power. He is in possession of his own right so far as he can in fact repel all force and avenge when he pleases any harm done to him, or, put comprehensively, so far as he has the power to live as his own mind prompts. 10. A man has another in his power when he holds him literally in bonds, or has deprived him of arms or of other means of self-defence or escape, or has filled him with fear, or by some favour has put him under so strong an obligation that he would rather gratify his benefactor than himself and order his life by that man's judgment than by his own. In the first two cases the power is over the other man's body only, not over his mind. In the second two he has brought mind as well as body under his right; but only while the other is actually in the grip of his fear or hope, for when either of these is absent he remains in possession of his own right.

11. A man's faculty of forming opinions can be under the right of another in a further way, namely, so far as his mind can be deceived by the other. This implies that a mind is in complete possession of its own right so far as it can in fact duly use its reason. Since human power has to be judged less by vigour of body than by strength of mind, those whose reason is strongest and are most guided by it are the ones who are most in possession of their own right. On this ground I call a man free so far as he is guided by reason, for he is then determined in his actions by causes which can be adequately understood through his own nature alone, even though he is being determined by them necessarily; for freedom does not (as was explained in Sect. 7) involve the denial of necessity in our actions, but on the contrary supposes it.

13. Si duo simul conveniant & vires iungant, plus simul possunt, & consequenter plus iuris in naturam simul habent, quam uterque solus, & quo plures necessitudines sic iunxerint suas eo omnes simul plus iuris habebunt. 14. Quatenus homines ira invidia aut aliquo odii adfectu conflictantur eatenus diverse trahuntur & invicem contrarii sunt, & propterea eo plus timendi quo plus possunt magisque callidi & astuti sunt quam reliqua animalia; & quia homines ut plurimum (ut in Art. 5 praec. Cap. diximus) his adfectibus natura sunt obnoxii, sunt ergo homines ex natura hostes; nam is mihi maxime hostis qui mihi maxime timendus & a quo mihi maxime cavendum est.

15. Cum autem in statu naturali tamdiu unusquisque sui iuris sit quamdiu sibi cavere potest ne ab alio opprimatur, & unus solus frustra ab omnibus sibi cavere conetur, hinc sequitur quamdiu ius humanum naturale uniuscuiusque potentia determinatur & uniuscuiusque est tamdiu nullum esse sed magis opinione quam re constare, quando quidem nulla eius obtinendi est securitas. Et certum est unumquemque tanto minus posse & consequenter tanto minus iuris habere quanto maiorem timendi causam habet. His accedit quod homines vix absque mutuo auxilio vitam sustentare & mentem colere possint; atque adeo concludimus ius naturae quod humani generis proprium est vix posse concipi nisi ubi homines iura habent communia, qui simul terras quas habitare & colere possunt sibi vindicare seseque munire vimque omnem repellere & ex communi omnium sententia vivere possunt. Nam quo plures in unum sic conveniunt eo omnes simul plus iuris habent; & si Scholastici hac de causa, quod scilicet homines in statu naturali vix sui iuris esse possunt, velint hominem animal sociale dicere, nihil habeo quod ipsis contradicam.

16. Ubi homines iura communia habent omnesque una veluti mente ducuntur, certum est eorum unumquemque tanto

13. If two men come together and combine their strength, they have more power together, and consequently more right over nature, than either has alone, and the more the men that so combine, the more right will they possess collectively.
14. So far as human beings are harassed by anger, envy or any sort of hatred, they are pulled in different directions and brought into conflict with one another; and they are all the more fearsome in being more powerful, skilful and cunning than all other living beings. Now since (as I said in Ch. I, Sect. 5) men are by nature liable in a high degree to those passions, they are by nature enemies to one another; and he is my greatest enemy whom I fear most, against whom I must be most on my guard.

15. Now since each man in his natural condition is in possession of his own right only so long as he can guard himself against being overpowered by anyone else, and since it is futile for a single man to try to guard himself against all the rest, we must infer that when the natural right of humans belongs only to individuals singly and is limited by the power of each, it is a nonentity, a notion rather than a fact, because there is no sure way of actualising it. Further, the more cause a man has for fear, the less power he has, and therefore the less right. Still further, it is scarcely possible for human beings to keep themselves alive and cultivate their minds unless they help one another. From these premisses I conclude that the right of nature that is peculiar to the human race is scarcely conceivable except where men have rights collectively, together with the power to defend the territory they dwell in and cultivate, to protect themselves, to repel all force, and to live by the common judgment of all. As I have said, the more men thus unite, the more right they have collectively. If the Schoolmen, in saying that man is a social being, mean that in the natural condition men can scarcely be in possession of their right, I have no objection to their formula.

16. Where men have rights collectively and are all guided by what may be called one mind, the right of each singly is in

minus habere iuris quanto reliqui simul ipso potentiores sunt, hoc est illum revera ius nullum in naturam habere praeter id quod ipsi commune concedit ius; ceterum quicquid ex communi consensu ipsi imperatur teneri exsequi vel iure ad id cogi. 17. Hoc ius, quod multitudinis potentia definitur, imperium appellari solet. Atque hoc is absolute tenet qui curam reipublicae ex communi consensu habet, nempe iura statuendi interpretandi & abolendi, urbes muniendi, de bello & pace decernendi &c. Quod si haec cura ad concilium pertineat quod ex communi multitudine componitur tum imperium democratia appellatur, si autem ex quibusdam tantum selectis aristocratia, & si denique reipublicae cura & consequenter imperium penes unum sit tum monarchia appellatur.

18. Ex his quae in hoc Capite ostendimus perspicuum nobis fit in statu naturali non dari peccatum, vel si quis peccat is sibi non alteri peccat; quando quidem nemo iure naturae alteri nisi velit morem gerere tenetur, nec aliquid bonum aut malum habere nisi quod ipse ex suo ingenio bonum aut malum esse decernit; & nihil absolute naturae iure prohibetur nisi quod nemo potest.... 19. Peccatum itaque non nisi in imperio concipi potest, ubi scilicet quid bonum & quid malum sit ex communi totius imperii iure decernitur & ubi nemo iure quicquam agit nisi quod ex communi decreto vel consensu agit. Id enim peccatum est quod iure fieri nequit sive quod iure prohibetur; obsequium autem est constans voluntas id exsequendi quod iure bonum est & ex communi decreto fieri debet.

20. Solemus tamen id etiam peccatum appellare quod contra sanae rationis dictamen fit, & obsequium constantem voluntatem moderandi appetitus ex rationis praescripto; quod omnino probarem si humana libertas in appetitus licentia & servitus in rationis imperio consisteret. Sed quia humana libertas eo maior est quo homo magis ratione duci & appetitus mode-

inverse proportion to the total power of all the rest, i.e. he has in fact no right over anything in nature except what the collective right allows him: in all else, whatever he is commanded by the collective mind he is under obligation to carry out, and can rightfully be forced to do so. 17. This right, defined by the power of a people, is usually called dominion. It resides wholly in whoever by common consent has the care of the State, i.e. who makes laws, interprets and repeals them, fortifies cities, decides war and peace, etc. If this office belongs to a council composed of the whole body of the people, the realm is called a democracy; if to a council composed only of selected persons, an aristocracy; if to a single man, a monarchy.

18. What I have said in this chapter should make it clear that in man's natural condition there is no such thing as wrongdoing; at any rate, if anyone does do wrong, he wrongs only himself; for by the right of nature no one is obliged to gratify another against his own will, or to deem anything good or bad except what his own cast of mind makes him think so, and by the right of nature nothing is forbidden except what nobody is able to do.... 19. Wrongdoing has no meaning except in a State; for there what is good and what bad are decreed by the collective right of the State as a whole, and there no individual has a right to do anything except what is prescribed by the communal agreement or decree. Wrongdoing, then, is what is contrary to law or forbidden by it. Obedience, on the other hand, is a settled will to do what rightful law declares to be good and communal decree makes obligatory.

20. It is customary, however, to use the term "wrongdoing" to indicate also what is contrary to the verdict of sound reason, and "obedience" to mean the settled will to control the appetites by reason. I would fully approve that usage if human freedom consisted in the unleashing of appetite, and servitude in domination by reason. But a man is all the more free the more he can be guided by reason and

rari potest, non possumus nisi admodum improprie vitam rationalem vocare obsequium, & peccatum id quod revera mentis impotentia non autem contra se ipsam licentia est & per quod homo servus potius quam liber potest dici. Vide Art. 7 & 11 huius Cap.

21. Verum enimvero quia ratio pietatem exercere & animo tranquillo & bono esse docet, quod non nisi in imperio fieri potest, & praeterea quia fieri nequit ut multitudo una veluti mente ducatur sicut in imperio requiritur nisi iura habeat quae ex rationis praescripto instituta sint, non ergo adeo improprie homines qui in imperio vivere consueverunt id peccatum vocant quod contra rationis dictamen fit, quando quidem optimi imperii iura ex rationis dictamine institui debent....

Cap. III

3. Si civitas alicui concedat ius & consequenter potestatem (nam alias verba tantum dedit) vivendi ex suo ingenio, eo ipso suo iure cedit & in eum transfert cui talem potestatem dedit. Si autem duobus aut pluribus hanc potestatem dedit, ut scilicet unusquisque ex suo ingenio vivat, eo ipso imperium divisit; & si denique unicuique civium hanc eandem potestatem dedit, eo ipso sese destruxit nec manet amplius civitas sed redeunt omnia ad statum naturalem — quae omnia ex praecedentibus manifestissima fiunt. Atque adeo sequitur nulla ratione posse concipi quod unicuique civi ex civitatis instituto liceat ex suo ingenio vivere, & consequenter hoc ius naturale, quod scilicet unusquisque sui iudex est, in statu civili necessario cessat. Dico expresse "ex civitatis instituto", nam ius naturae uniuscuiusque (si recte rem perpendamus) in statu civili non cessat. Homo namque tam in statu naturali quam civili ex legibus suae naturae agit suaeque utilitati consulit. Homo inquam in utroque statu spe aut metu ducitur ad hoc

control his appetites. Therefore we cannot, without great impropriety, apply the term "obedience" to the rational life, and "wrongdoing" to what is not a liberty of the mind to act against itself but really a mental powerlessness, for which a man can be called servile rather than free (see Sects. 7 & 11).

21. Nevertheless, because reason teaches us to behave morally, and to have a peaceable and kindly disposition, which is possible only in a State; and because a large body of people cannot be guided by, so to speak, a single mind, as is required in a State, unless they have laws that are founded on what is enjoined by reason: we may say that men accustomed to living under political rule are not greatly misusing the term "wrongdoing" when they apply it to what is against the verdict of reason, for it is on the direction of reason that the laws of the best kind of State have to rest....

CH. III. THE RIGHT OF THE SOVEREIGN POWER OVER SUBJECTS

3. If a State grants to anyone the right, and therefore the power (for otherwise the granting is merely verbal), to live as he himself thinks fit, it thereby relinquishes its own right and transfers it to that person. If it gives that power to two or more persons, it thereby divides the ruling authority. If it gives that power to every citizen singly, it thereby destroys itself, and then, there being no longer a State, everything reverts to the natural condition. All this follows quite clearly from what has been already said. In consequence, it is self-contradictory to think of every citizen as being allowed *by law* to live as he himself thinks fit: the natural right of everyone to be the judge of his own actions necessarily lapses in a politically ordered society. I have been careful to say "by law" because the natural right of the individual does not in fact lapse in a political society. In both the natural and the political orders a man acts in accordance with the laws of his nature and consults his own interest. In both orders alike he is moved to do one thing or to refrain from

aut illud agendum vel omittendum. Sed praecipua inter utrumque statum differentia est quod in statu civili omnes eadem metuant & omnibus una eademque securitatis sit causa & vivendi ratio, quod sane iudicandi facultatem uniuscuiusque non tollit. Qui enim omnibus civitatis mandatis obtemperare constituit, sive eius potentiam metuit vel quia tranquillitatem amat, is profecto suae securitati suaeque utilitati ex suo ingenio consulit.

4. Praeterea concipere etiam non possumus quod unicuique civi liceat civitatis decreta seu iura interpretari. Nam si hoc unicuique liceret, eo ipso sui iudex esset, quando quidem unusquisque facta sua specie iuris nullo negotio excusare seu adornare posset & consequenter ex suo ingenio vitam institueret, quod (per Art. praeced.) est absurdum.

5. Videmus itaque unumquemque civem non sui sed civitatis iuris esse, cuius omnia mandata tenetur exsequi, nec ullum habere ius decernendi quid aequum quid iniquum quid pium quidve impium sit; sed contra quia imperii corpus una veluti mente duci debet & consequenter civitatis voluntas pro omnium voluntate habenda est, id quod civitas iustum & bonum esse decernit tamquam ab unoquoque decretum esse censendum est; atque adeo quamvis subditus civitatis decreta iniqua esse censeat tenetur nihilo minus eadem exsequi.

6. At obici potest an non contra rationis dictamen est se alterius iudicio omnino subicere, & consequenter an status civilis rationi non repugnat; ex quo sequeretur statum civilem irrationalem esse nec posse creari nisi ab hominibus ratione destitutis, at minime ab iis qui ratione ducuntur. Sed quoniam ratio nihil contra naturam docet, non potest ergo sana ratio dictare ut unusquisque sui iuris maneat quamdiu homines adfectibus sunt obnoxii, hoc est ratio hoc posse fieri negat. Adde quod ratio omnino docet pacem quaerere, quae quidem obtineri nequit nisi communia civitatis iura inviolata serventur; at-

doing another by either hope or fear. The chief difference between the two orders is that in the political order all fear the same things, and all have one and the same ground of security and one and the same rule of life. But this does not, of course, take away the individual's power of forming his own judgments; for anyone who resolves to obey all the commands of the State, whether through fear of its power or for love of peace, is still following his own view of his security and advantage.

4. It is also self-contradictory to think of every citizen as being allowed to *interpret* the laws or rights of the State in his own way. If he were allowed to do so, he would thereby be his own judge, since he would then have no difficulty in excusing or dressing up all his actions with an appearance of legality, and would thus order his life in his own way—which is (by the previous Section) absurd.

5. It is evident, then, that everybody, when a citizen, has no right of his own but is under the right of the State, obliged to carry out all its commands. He has no right to decide what is equitable and what inequitable, what moral or immoral. On the contrary, because the political body must be directed as by a single mind and the will of the State be regarded as the will of all, what the State decides to be just and good must be considered as having been so decided by every citizen. However inequitable a subject may believe the State's decisions to be, he is none the less under obligation to carry them out.

6. It may be objected that it is against the voice of reason to subject oneself completely to the judgment of someone else, and consequently that the political order is irrational, so that it could be set up only by men lacking reason, not by those who are guided by it. Now reason teaches nothing contrary to nature; therefore it cannot declare, indeed it denies, that everyone should retain his individual right when everyone is subject to passions. Also, the most general precept of reason is that we should seek peace, and this cannot be got unless the corporate laws or rights of the State are kept inviolate;

que adeo quo homo ratione magis ducitur, hoc est (per Art. 11 praeced. Cap.) quo magis liber est, eo constantius civitatis iura servabit & summae potestatis cuius subditus est mandata exsequetur. Ad quod accedit quod status civilis naturaliter instituitur ad metum communem adimendum & communes miserias propellendum, ac proinde id maxime intendit quod unusquisque qui ratione ducitur in statu naturali conaretur, sed frustra. Quapropter si homini qui ratione ducitur id aliquando ex civitatis mandato faciendum est quod rationi repugnare novit, id damnum longe compensatur bono quod ex ipso statu civili haurit. Nam rationis etiam lex est ut ex duobus malis minus eligatur; ac proinde concludere possumus neminem quicquam contra suae rationis praescriptum agere quatenus id agit quod iure civitatis faciendum est; quod nobis facilius unusquisque concedet postquam explicuerimus quousque civitatis potentia & consequenter ius se extendit.

7. Nam considerandum primum venit quod sicuti in statu naturali ille homo maxime potens maximeque sui iuris est qui ratione ducitur, sic etiam illa civitas maxime erit potens & maxime sui iuris quae ratione fundatur & dirigitur. Nam civitatis ius potentia multitudinis quae una veluti mente ducitur determinatur. At haec animorum unio concipi nulla ratione posset nisi civitas id ipsum maxime intendat quod sana ratio omnibus hominibus utile esse docet.

8. Secundo venit etiam considerandum quod subditi eatenus non sui sed civitatis iuris sint quatenus eius potentiam seu minas metuunt vel quatenus statum civilem amant (per Art. 10 praeced. Cap.). Ex quo sequitur quod ea omnia ad quae agenda nemo praemiis aut minis induci potest ad iura civitatis non pertineant. Ex. gr. iudicandi facultate nemo cedere potest. Quibus enim praemiis aut minis induci potest homo ut credat totum

therefore the more a person is guided by reason, i.e. the freer he is (Ch. II, Sect. 11), the more consistently will he respect the rights and carry out the commands of the State of which he is a subject. Furthermore, the political order is established by nature for the purpose of taking away the fear and warding off the distresses to which all humans are exposed: therefore its chief end is the very one which everybody who is guided by reason strives after, though in vain, in man's natural condition. If, then, any individual who has put himself under the guidance of reason finds that sometimes he is commanded by the State to do what he knows to be contrary to reason, this grievance is more than balanced by the good he gets from there being a political order at all. That when we are faced with two evils we should choose the lesser is itself a law of reason. From these several considerations we can draw the general conclusion that nobody is acting against the injunction of his reason when he is doing what the law of the State requires. This will be readily granted when I have explained how far the State's power, and therefore its right, extends.

7. First, just as in man's natural condition that person is the most powerful and in the fullest possession of his individual right who is guided by reason, so too that State will be the most powerful and in the fullest possession of its right which is established and directed by reason. Now the right of a State is bounded by the power of a people that is led by what may be called a single mind, and such a union of minds is impossible unless the State's chief aim is what sound reason pronounces to be the good of all the citizens.

8. Secondly, subjects are living not by their own right but under the State's right so far as they fear its power or threats, or so far as they are fond of society as politically organised (by Ch. II, Sect. 10). It follows logically that what no one can be induced to do by rewards or threats is beyond the scope of the right of the State. E.g. nobody can relinquish his power of forming his own judgments. Now, by what rewards or threats can anybody be induced to believe that the

non esse sua parte maius, aut quod Deus non exsistat, aut quod corpus quod videt finitum ens infinitum esse credat, & absolute ut aliquid contra id quod sentit vel cogitat credat? Sic etiam quibus praemiis aut minis induci potest homo ut amet quem odit vel ut odio habeat quem amat? Atque huc etiam illa referenda sunt a quibus humana natura ita abhorret ut ipsa omni malo peiora habeat, ut quod homo testem contra se agat, ut se cruciet, ut parentes interficiat suos, ut mortem vitare non conetur & similia, ad quae nemo praemiis nec minis induci potest. Quod si tamen dicere velimus civitatem ius sive potestatem habere talia imperandi, id nullo alio sensu poterimus concipere nisi quo quis diceret hominem iure posse insanire & delirare; quid enim aliud nisi delirium ius illud esset cui nemo adstrictus esse potest? Atque hic de iis expresse loquor quae iuris civitatis esse nequeunt & a quibus natura humana plerumque abhorret. Nam quod stultus aut vesanus nullis praemiis neque minis induci possit ad exsequenda mandata, & quod unus aut alter ex eo quod huic aut illi religioni addictus sit imperii iura omni malo peiora iudicat, iura tamen civitatis irrita non sunt, quando quidem iisdem plerique cives continentur; ac proinde quia ii qui nihil timent neque sperant eatenus sui iuris sunt, sunt ergo imperii hostes, quos iure cohibere licet.

9. Tertio denique considerandum venit ad civitatis ius ea minus pertinere quae plurimi indignantur. Nam certum est homines naturae ductu in unum conspirare vel propter communem metum vel desiderio damnum aliquod commune ulciscendi; & quia ius civitatis communi multitudinis potentia definitur, certum est potentiam civitatis & ius eatenus minui quatenus ipsa causas praebet ut plures in unum conspirent. Habet certe civitas quaedam sibi metuenda, & sicut unusquisque civis sive homo in statu naturali sic civitas eo minus sui iuris est quo maiorem timendi causam habet. Atque haec de iure summarum potestatum in subditos....

whole is not greater than the part, or that there is no God, or that a body which he sees to be finite is infinite—in general, that anything is contrary to what he perceives or knows it to be? Similarly, what rewards or threats can make a man love someone he hates, or hate someone he loves? Of the same kind too are the actions which human nature finds so abhorrent that it counts them the worst of all evils, such as bearing witness against oneself, torturing oneself, killing one's parents, not trying to avoid death: nobody can be led to do any of these by either rewards or threats. To say that the State has the right or power to command such things is as absurd as to say that a man can have the right to be mad. A right that cannot be obligatory on anybody is itself a mad idea. I am here speaking only of what *cannot* fall under the right of the State, and of what is abhorrent to human nature in general. There are, indeed, fools and madmen who cannot by any rewards or threats be brought to fulfil the requirements of the law, and there are a few people who, under the scruple of some religion or sect, believe that the laws of the State are the worst of all evils. But the State's laws are not thereby invalidated or made ineffective, for they do control the greater part of the citizens. The conclusion to be drawn is that those who are not moved by fear or hope, remaining to that extent in possession of their own right, are enemies of the State, and therefore can rightfully be repressed by it.

9. Thirdly, laws or actions that drive most of the subjects to anger do not fall within the State's right. Men cannot help banding together when they have a common fear or to avenge a common injury; and since the State's right is defined and bounded by the people's collective power, the power and right of the State are lessened in proportion as it provokes more and more of the citizens to join in conspiracy against it. Even a State itself has things to fear, and, like the individual citizen and like men in their natural condition, the greater its cause for fear the less is it in effective possession of its right. So much for the right of the Sovereign Power over subjects....

10. Nam obici nobis potest an status civilis & subditorum oboedientia qualem in statu civili requiri ostendimus non tollat religionem qua Deum colere tenemur. Sed si rem ipsam perpendamus nihil reperiemus quod possit scrupulum inicere. Mens enim quatenus ratione utitur non summarum potestatum sed sui iuris est (per Art. 11 Cap. praeced.). Atque adeo vera Dei cognitio & amor nullius imperio subici potest, ut nec erga proximum caritas; & si praeterea consideremus summum caritatis exercitium esse illud quod ad pacem tuendam & concordiam conciliandam fit, non dubitabimus illum revera suo officio functum esse qui unicuique tantum auxilii fert quantum iura civitatis, hoc est concordia & tranquillitas, concedunt. Ad externos cultus quod attinet certum est illos ad veram Dei cognitionem & amorem qui ex ea necessario sequitur, nihil prorsus iuvare nec nocere posse; atque adeo non tanti faciendi sunt ut propter ipsos pax & tranquillitas publica perturbari mereatur....

CAP. IV

4. Sed quaeri solet an summa potestas legibus adstricta sit & consequenter an peccare possit. Verum quoniam legis & peccati nomina non tantum civitatis iura sed etiam omnium rerum naturalium & apprime rationis communes regulas respicere solent, non possumus absolute dicere civitatem nullis adstrictam esse legibus seu peccare non posse. Nam si civitas nullis legibus seu regulis sine quibus civitas non esset civitas adstricta esset, tum civitas non ut res naturalis sed ut chimaera esset contemplanda. Peccat ergo civitas quando ea agit vel fieri patitur quae causa esse possunt ipsius ruinae, atque tum eandem eo sensu peccare dicimus quo philosophi vel medici naturam peccare dicunt, & hoc sensu dicere possumus civita-

10. I may well be asked if the political order, requiring the high degree of obedience which I have expounded, abolishes the religious duty to worship God. We have only to examine the point directly to see that there is no ground for uneasiness. So far as the mind makes use of reason it is acting not under the right of the Sovereign Power but under its own (Ch. II, Sect. 11). Therefore the true knowledge and love of God cannot be subject to any ruler's command, just as charity to one's neighbour cannot; and if we bear in mind that the greatest expression of charity is the seeking of peace and concord, we cannot have any doubt that a man is truly doing his duty who gives to each of his fellows as much help as the laws of the State (in effect, its concord and peace) allow. As for the external rites of religion, these have no bearing at all, either helpful or hurtful, on the true knowledge of God and on the love that necessarily follows from it, and consequently they are not to be valued so highly as to make differences of opinion about them a justification for disturbing the public peace....

CH. IV. IN WHAT SENSE THE SOVEREIGN POWER CAN DO WRONG

4. It is usual to ask whether a Sovereign Power is bound by laws, and thus capable of wrongdoing. An unqualified negative answer cannot be given because the terms "law" and "wrongdoing" are customarily used with reference not only to the laws of a State but also to the general laws of nature and especially the general rules of reason. Now if a State were not bound by the laws or rules without which it would not be a State, it would have to be thought of not as a natural reality but as a mere fantasy. A State does wrong, therefore, when it does, or allows its subjects to do, anything that can be the cause of its own downfall. It is then doing wrong in the sense in which scientists and doctors say that nature does wrong; and it is in this sense we can say that a State does

115

tem peccare quando contra rationis dictamen aliquid agit. Est enim civitas tum maxime sui iuris quando ex dictamine rationis agit; quatenus igitur contra rationem agit eatenus sibi deficit seu peccat. Atque haec clarius intellegi poterunt si consideremus quod cum dicimus unumquemque posse de re quae sui iuris est statuere quicquid velit, haec potestas non sola agentis potentia sed etiam ipsius patientis aptitudine definiri debet. Si enim ex. gr. dico me iure posse de hac mensa quicquid velim facere, non hercle intellego quod ius habeam efficiendi ut haec mensa herbam comedat. Sic etiam tametsi dicimus homines non sui sed civitatis iuris esse, non intellegemus quod homines naturam humanam amittant & aliam induant; atque adeo quod civitas ius habeat efficiendi ut homines volent vel, quod aeque impossibile est, ut homines cum honore aspiciant ea quae risum movent vel nauseam; sed quod quaedam circumstantiae occurrant quibus positis ponitur subditorum erga civitatem reverentia & metus, & quibus sublatis metus & reverentia & cum his civitas una tollitur. Civitas itaque, ut sui iuris sit, metus & reverentiae causas servare tenetur, alias civitas esse desinit....

5. Videmus itaque quo sensu dicere possumus civitatem legibus teneri & peccare posse. Verum si per legem intellegamus ius civile, quod ipso iure civili vindicari potest, & peccatum id quod iure civili fieri prohibetur, hoc est si haec nomina genuino sensu sumantur, nulla ratione dicere possumus civitatem legibus adstrictam esse aut posse peccare. Nam regulae & causae metus & reverentiae, quas civitas sui causa servare tenetur, non ad iura civilia sed ad ius naturale spectant, quando quidem non iure civili sed iure belli vindicari possunt; & civitas nulla alia ratione iisdem tenetur quam homo in statu naturali, ut sui iuris esse possit sive ne sibi hostis sit, cavere

116

wrong when it does anything against the voice of reason. For a State is most fully in possession of its own right when it acts under the direction of that voice, and therefore when it acts against this it is failing to fulfil its function, i.e. is doing wrong. The point will become clearer if we note that while, according to my contention, everyone has the power to do as he pleases in any matter within his right, his power is to be thought of as limited not simply by his own capability but also by the nature of what he is acting on. E.g. if I say that I have the right to do what I like with this table, I do not, of course, mean that I have the right to make it eat grass. Similarly, in saying that men act not by their own right but by the right of the State I do not mean that they lose their human nature and put on a different one, and that therefore the State has the right to make them fly or—for this is just as impossible—to make them honour what is ridiculous or disgusting. I mean that there are certain conjunctions of circumstance which when realised evoke in subjects respect for the State and fear of it, and in the absence of which there is no fear, no respect, and therefore no State. A State, then, to be in possession of its right, is obliged to maintain the conditions that produce fear and respect, for otherwise it ceases to be a State....

5. Such is the sense in which we are able to say that the State is bound by law and can do wrong. If, however, by "law" we mean civil law, which can be enforced only by the civil authority itself, and by "wrongdoing" mean what is forbidden by civil law, so taking the two terms in their proper sense, we are entirely precluded from saying that the State is bound by laws and can do wrong. The rules that concern and the conditions that produce the fear and respect which a State is obliged to maintain in order to maintain itself, fall within the sphere not of civil laws but of natural right, for they cannot be enforced by civil law but only by the right of war. A State is bound by them only in the sense in which a man in the natural condition is bound to be careful not to take his own

tenetur ne se ipsum interficiat, quae sane cautio non obsequium sed humanae naturae libertas est. At iura civilia pendent a solo civitatis decreto, atque haec nemini nisi sibi, ut scilicet libera maneat, morem gerere tenetur, nec aliud bonum aut malum habere nisi quod ipsa sibi bonum aut malum esse decernit; ac proinde non tantum ius habet sese vindicandi leges condendi & interpretandi sed etiam easdem abrogandi, & reo cuicumque ex plenitudine potentiae condonandi.

6. Contractus seu leges quibus multitudo ius suum in unum concilium vel hominem transferunt non dubium est quin violari debeant quando communis salutis interest easdem violare. At iudicium de hac re, an scilicet communis salutis intersit easdem violare an secus, nemo privatus sed is tantum qui imperium tenet iure ferre potest; ergo iure civili is solus qui imperium tenet earum leges interpres manet. Ad quod accedit quod nullus privatus easdem iure vindicare possit; atque adeo eum qui imperium tenet revera non obligant. Quod si tamen eius naturae sint ut violari nequeant nisi simul civitatis robur debilitetur, hoc est nisi simul plerorumque civium communis metus in indignationem vertatur, eo ipso civitas dissolvitur & contractus cessat, qui propterea non iure civili sed iure belli vindicatur. Atque adeo is qui imperium tenet nulla etiam alia de causa huius contractus condiciones servare tenetur quam homo in statu naturali, ne sibi hostis sit, tenetur cavere ne se ipsum interficiat.

CAP. V

2. Qualis autem optimus cuiuscumque imperii sit status facile ex fine status civilis cognoscitur, qui scilicet nullus alius est quam pax vitaeque securitas. Ac proinde illud imperium optimum est ubi homines concorditer vitam transigunt & cuius iura inviolata servantur. Nam certum est quod seditiones bella

life if he is to preserve his natural right and not be his own enemy—a precaution which is obviously not subservience but an expression of man's natural freedom. Civil laws, on the contrary, depend entirely on the decision of the State, and the State, in order to remain free to fulfil its function, is bound to consider nothing but itself, and to regard nothing as good or bad except what it deems to be so to itself. Consequently, it possesses the right not only to uphold itself, to enact laws and interpret them, but also to revoke them, and, in addition, out of its plenary power, to pardon any offender.

6. The compact or laws by which a people transfers its right to a single council or man should certainly be broken when the general welfare requires it to do so. But the decision whether or no the general welfare does require it can be rightfully taken only by the ruling authority, not by any private citizen. Hence, by civil right the ruling authority remains the sole interpreter of those laws. Further, no private citizen has the right to enforce them, so that they are not in fact binding on the ruling authority. If, however, they are of such a kind that they cannot be broken without crippling the State's power, by turning the fear of most of the citizens into indignation, any breach of them would dissolve the State and thereby bring the compact to an end. The compact is thus enforceable not by civil law but by the right of war. A ruler is bound to observe the compact, then, for one reason only, the same as that which binds an individual in the natural condition not to kill himself, namely, lest he should be his own enemy.

CH. V. THE GENERAL CHARACTERISTICS OF THE GOOD STATE

2. What the best condition is of any form of State can be inferred directly from the goal of the political kind of social order—simply peace and security of life. The best State is therefore one in which the people live in concord and the laws are obeyed. Now revolts, armed strife, and disregard or

legumque contemptio sive violatio non tam subditorum malitiae quam pravo imperii statui imputanda sunt. Homines enim civiles non nascuntur sed fiunt. Hominum praeterea naturales adfectus ubique iidem sunt. Si itaque in una civitate malitia magis regnat pluraque peccata committuntur quam in alia, certum est id ex eo oriri quod talis civitas non satis concordiae providerit nec iura satis prudenter instituerit, & consequenter neque ius civitatis absolutum obtinuerit. Status enim civilis qui seditionum causas non abstulit & ubi bellum continuo timendum & ubi denique leges frequenter violantur non multum ab ipso naturali statu differt, ubi unusquisque ex suo ingenio magno vitae periculo vivit.

4. Civitas cuius subditi metu territi arma non capiunt potius dicenda est quod sine bello sit quam quod pacem habeat. Pax enim non belli privatio sed virtus est, quae ex animi fortitudine oritur; est namque obsequium constans voluntas id exsequendi quod ex communi civitatis decreto fieri debet. Illa praeterea civitas cuius pax a subditorum inertia pendet, qui scilicet veluti pecora ducuntur ut tantum servire discant, rectius solitudo quam civitas dici potest.

5. Cum ergo dicimus illud imperium optimum esse ubi homines concorditer vitam transigunt, vitam humanam intellego, quae non sola sanguinis circulatione & aliis quae omnibus animalibus sunt communia sed quae maxime ratione, vera mentis virtute & vita, definitur.

6. Sed notandum imperium quod in hunc finem institui dixi a me intellegi id quod multitudo libera instituit, non autem id quod in multitudinem iure belli acquiritur. Libera enim multitudo maiori spe quam metu, subacta autem maiori metu quam spe ducitur. Quippe illa vitam colere, haec autem mortem tantummodo vitare studet; illa inquam sibi vivere studet, haec victoris esse cogitur, unde hanc servire illam liberam esse dicimus. Finis itaque imperii quod aliquis iure belli adipiscitur est dominari, & servos potius quam subditos habere. Et quam-

breaking of the laws must be attributed to some perversity in the government rather than to wickedness in the subjects; for men are not born citizens, but have to be made such. Moreover, human passions are the same everywhere. If, then, wickedness and crime are more prevalent in one State than in another, the cause must be that that State has not sufficiently provided the conditions that favour concord, and has not drawn up its laws with sufficient foresight; which means that it has not in fact laid hold of the absolute right of a State to rule. A political order in which the causes of revolts have not been removed, and the fear of armed strife is ever present, and the laws are often broken, differs little from the natural condition in which everybody behaves as he pleases but at great peril to his life.

4. A State whose subjects are kept from armed revolt by sheer fear is better said to be without strife than to be at peace; for peace is not the mere absence of strife but a positive excellence, which comes from a certain strength of mind, civic obedience being a firm resoluteness to do what the decree of the State enjoins. A State in which peace depends on the torpor of the subjects, these being led like sheep and learning only to be servile, is more rightly called a steppe than a State.

5. In saying that the best State is one in which life is harmonious I mean, then, not a merely animal but a human life, defined chiefly by reason, which is the real life and excellence of a mind.

6. I must point out that by a State instituted for this end I mean one that has been instituted by a free people, not a dominion over the people that has been got by the right of war. A free people is governed more by hope than fear, a conquered one more by fear than hope, and the former is bent on developing its life, the latter only on avoiding death. The former, I maintain, is engaged in living for itself, whereas the latter lives under the compulsion of its conquerors, so that this is in servitude and that free. Thus the aim of a State acquired by the right of war is to dominate, to have slaves

vis inter imperium quod a libera multitudine creatur, & illud quod iure belli acquiritur, si ad utriusque ius in genere attendamus, nulla essentialis detur differentia, finem tamen, ut iam ostendimus, & praeterea media quibus unumquodque conservari debeat admodum diversa habent.

rather than subjects. Although there is no essential difference between the two kinds of State in the right of rule considered in its most general sense, there is a very great difference not only between their aims, as I have just pointed out, but also between the means by which they have to preserve themselves.

APPENDIX

FURTHER RELEVANT EXTRACTS

I. From Spinoza's Letters

1665, to Henry Oldenburg. Not in the Opera Posthuma. Ep. 30 in Heidelberg edition of the Opera.

...I am at present writing a treatise [*Theol.-Pol.*] that will show how I interpret Scripture. My reasons for doing so are the following. 1. The prejudices of the theologians. For I am well aware that it is those prejudices that do more than anything else to keep men from the study of philosophy. I am therefore taking pains to expose them, and to clear them out of the minds of people of good education. 2. The opinion which the mass of the people have of me. They are forever charging me with atheism. I cannot help doing my best to dispel that opinion too. 3. Freedom to philosophise and to declare our views. I want to give a complete vindication of such freedom, for in this country, through the excessive influence and insolence of the preachers, it is in one way or another being suppressed...

1671, Feb. 17, addressee unknown. Ep. 47 (44 in Heidelberg ed.).

When Professor...... visited me recently, he told me among other things that he had heard that my *Theologico-Political Treatise* had been translated into Dutch, and that someone,

whose name he did not know, was intending to have it printed. I beg you to inquire thoroughly into the matter, and if possible to prevent the printing. This is not my request only but also that of many of my friends and acquaintances, who would not like to see the book publicly prohibited, as it certainly will be if it appears in Dutch. I am sure you will do me and our cause this service....[1]

1675, to Henry Oldenburg. Ep. 19 (68 in Heidelberg ed.).

When I received your letter of July 22 I was setting out for Amsterdam in order to arrange for the printing of the book *Ethics* about which I had written to you. While I was negotiating, a rumour ran round there that a book by me about God was actually in the press, in which I try to prove that there is no God. The rumour was widely believed. Certain theologians (who perhaps had started it) used it as a ground for laying a complaint about me before the Prince and magistrates. Besides, the dull-headed Cartesians, generally thought to be well disposed towards me and now taking a chance of removing this imputation, began to denounce my views and writings, everywhere and constantly, and are doing so still.[2] When from reliable sources I heard these things, and also that the theologians were on all sides plotting against me, I decided to postpone the publication I was arranging until I could see what turn events would take, and to let you know what plan I would then follow. Every day, however, the situation seems to take a turn for the worse, and I am not sure what to do. In the meantime, I do not want your letter to remain any longer unanswered. First, let me thank you deeply for your friendly warning. I need, however, some specification of it, so that I may know which the doctrines are

---

[1] The translation referred to was not published until 1693.
[2] On these complaints and denunciations see J. Freudenthal, *Spinoza, Leben und Lehre* (2nd ed., ed. by C. Gebhardt, 1927, Heidelberg), pp. 233-8.

that, in your opinion, seem to unsettle the practice of piety; for I hold that whatever I see to be consonant with reason is of the utmost value to virtue. Secondly, I would like you to point out to me, if it is not too much trouble, the passages in the *Theologico-Political Treatise* which have caused misgivings to the learned; for I wish to elucidate that treatise with some notes [1], and if possible to remove premature judgments that have been made on it...

1675, to Henry Oldenburg. Ep. 21 (73 in Heidelberg ed.).

I received your too brief letter of Nov. 15 last Saturday. In it you merely point out the passages in the *Theologico-Political Treatise* that vex readers. I had hoped you would tell me what in any of those passages the views were that, as you warned me earlier, seemed to them to unsettle the practice of piety. However, I will make my meaning clear on the three subjects you mention. On the first, I must say that I hold a view about God and Nature very different from that which the modern Christians usually stand for. I declare that God is (to use the technical terms) the "immanent" not the "transient" cause of all things. I mean that I affirm with Paul that in God all things move and have their being; perhaps also with all the ancient philosophers, though I conceive it somewhat differently; and, I venture to add, with all the ancient Jews as well, so far as may be gathered from some of the traditions, allowing that these have suffered much distortion. But those who think that the *Theologico-Political Treatise* rests on the identification of God and Nature are altogether wide of the mark, for they are here taking Nature to mean a determinate mass, or corporeal matter... [2].

---

[1] No notes were published by Spinoza, but a number have come to us from several sources (see *Opera*, Heidelberg ed., vol. III, pp. 382ff. and 251ff.). They are on the religious passages.

[2] See above, p. *xxxii*, note.

II. From the *Ethics*

Part IV, prop. 18, note.

It is impossible for us ever to make ourselves able to survive independently of, or to live out of relation with, anything external to ourselves; and as for the mind, if it were isolated, knowing nothing beyond itself, our understanding would certainly be more imperfect. There are, then, many things outside us that are useful to us, and consequently to be desired. Now we cannot imagine any of them to be more useful than those that are completely consonant with our own nature. For instance, if two individual things entirely the same in nature be joined together, they become a new individual twice as strong as each is separately. There is nothing more advantageous to men, then, than other men; that is, they cannot desire anything better for their survival than an agreement among all of them concerning all matters, to make the minds and bodies of all become as it were a single mind and a single body, to do their utmost together to preserve themselves, and together to seek the good of all. It follows that men who in seeking what is beneficial to themselves are guided by reason desire for themselves only what they desire for the rest, and that therefore such men are just, trustworthy and honourable.

These are the verdicts of reason which, before I proceed to prove them at length, I have set forth briefly in order to gain the attention of those who think that the principle that everybody cannot but seek his own benefit is the ground not of virtue and piety but of impiety.

Part IV, prop. 35, note.

Men rarely live by reason; on the contrary, their frame of mind makes them on the whole mutually hostile and annoying. Nevertheless, they can hardly manage to live alone. Consequently, the old definition that man is a social animal has been widely and strongly approved. It certainly is the fact that far more benefit than hurt comes from living together

in fellowship. Let the satirists ridicule human affairs as they please, and theologians execrate them, and pessimists praise to the skies the primitive and boorish level of life, despising men and admiring beasts [1]. Nevertheless, men will continue to find that by mutual help they will get what they need far more easily, and that only by joining their forces will they be able to avoid the dangers that everywhere hang over them. Not to mention that it is better, more worthy of knowledge, to have men in view than beasts.

Part IV, prop. 37, note 2.

Every man exists by the supreme right of nature, and consequently by that same right does those things that proceed necessarily from his nature. By that right, then, every man judges what is good and what bad, is his own avenger, and tries to preserve what he likes and to destroy what he hates. If, however, men lived by reason, each would secure that right without any hurt to anyone else; but because they are liable to emotions, which are far stronger than our rational power or virtue, they are often pulled apart from one another, and are hostile even though they are in need of mutual help. If, then, they are to live together in concord and be helpful to one another, they must surrender their natural right and so make themselves harmless to one another, each undertaking to do nothing that would injure anyone else. The principle on which men liable to emotions, and changeable and fickle, can make themselves mutually harmless and trustworthy, is evident from proposition 7 of this Part and proposition 39 of Part III, namely, that no emotion can be restrained except by one stronger and opposite, and that everybody refrains from injury through fear of a greater injury to himself. By this law [of nature] a society can be held firmly together, provided it appropriates to itself the right each individual has of being

---

[1] Rousseau's criticism of civilisation (*Discours de l'inégalité*, 1755) was original only in the brilliance of its literary expression.

his own champion and of deciding for himself what is good and what bad — a society that thereby has the power to prescribe a common pattern of life, and to institute laws, making these effective not by appealing to reason (since this cannot restrain emotion) but by threats of punishment. Such a society, held together by laws and the power to maintain itself, is called a State, and those who are defended by its authority are called citizens.

From all this it is clear that in the natural condition of man there is nothing that is good or bad by common consent, since there everyone considers only his own advantage, deciding what is good and what bad as his own mind leads him and merely with reference to his own profit; that nobody is under any sort of law to obey anyone other than himself; and therefore that in the natural condition the notion of wrongdoing has no place, but has meaning only at the level of political society, where what is good and what bad are decided by common consent, and where everyone is required to give obedience to the State. Wrongdoing is therefore nothing but disobedience to the State, and is accordingly punished by nothing but the authority of the State; and merit, on the other hand, is what is attributed to a citizen for obedience, because in virtue of this he is deemed worthy of the benefits which the State provides.

Moreover, in the natural condition nobody is by common acknowledgement the owner of anything; and there is nothing in nature that can be said to belong to this person and not to that. Everything there belongs to everybody, so that it is meaningless to speak of allowing each man to have his own or of taking away what belongs to him. That is, in the natural condition no deed can be called just or unjust. This distinction has meaning only in a State, where a common mind decides what belongs to this man and what to that. Evidently, then, just and unjust, wrongdoing and merit, are ideas that are externally conditioned, not properties that directly express the mind's own nature.

PRINTED IN ITALY
BY S.T.I.A.V.
FIRENZE

PHILOSOPHY AND WORLD COMMUNITY

Volumes published up to date:

In English: *The Edicts of Asoka.* Edited and translated by N. A. Nikam and R. McKeon. Chicago, University of Chicago Press, 1959. Cloth $1.75.

In German: JOHN LOCKE, *Ein Brief über Toleranz.* Übersetzt, eingeleitet und in Anmerkungen erläutert von Julius Ebbinghaus. Hamburg, Felix Meiner, 1957. Paper $1.50; cloth $2.25.

In Italian: *Gli Editti di Asoka.* Traduzione e introduzione di G. Pugliese Carratelli. Premessa di Humayun Kabir. Firenze, La Nuova Italia Editrice, 1960. $1.00.

SEBASTIANO CASTELLIONE, *Fede, Dubbio e Tolleranza.* Pagine scelte e tradotte da Giorgio Radetti. Firenze, La Nuova Italia Editrice, 1960. $1.65.

JOHN LOCKE, *Lettera sulla tolleranza.* Testo latino e versione italiana. Premessa di R. Klibansky. Introduzione di E. de Marchi. Traduzione di L. Formigari. Firenze, La Nuova Italia Editrice, 1961. $1.50.

In course of publication:

In French: JOHN LOCKE, *Lettre sur la tolérance,* edited and translated by R. Polin. Foreword by R. Klibansky. Montreal, Mario Casalini.

In Spanish: JOHN LOCKE, *Carta sobre la tolerancia,* edited and translated by A. Waismann. Foreword by R. Klibansky. Montreal, Mario Casalini.

Further volumes are being prepared.